GROUNDED
N LOVE

acramental Theology in
1 Ecumenical Perspective

rans Jozef van Beeck, S.J.

RSITY
OF
CA

GROUNDED IN LOVE

Sacramental Theology
in an Ecumenical Perspective

Frans Jozef van Beeck, S.J.
///

i

Copyright © 1981 by

Frans Jozef van Beeck

University Press of America, Inc.

P.O. Box 19101, Washington, D.C. 20036

Printed in the United States of America

ISBN: 0-8191-2041-3 (Perfect)

ISBN: 0-8191-2040-6 (Cloth)

Imprimi potest:

Edward M. O'Flaherty, S.J.

Provincial, New England Province,

February 24, 1981

Library of Congress Catalog Card Number: 81-40117

For Mark Santer —
  " bonum opus desiderat "

ACKNOWLEDGMENTS

Credit for the happy completion of this typescript must go in three directions. There was the September 1 contract deadline, sweetened by the courtesy of Helen Hudson of University Press of America. There was the friendship, and the accuracy, of Brenda Andrews Natchek, who read the proofs and put the index together. (I insist on claiming full credit for my erratic way of breaking off words at the ends of lines.) Finally, there was a temporary inability on my part, due to extraneous factors, to do much in the way of more creative work.

Boston College, Summer of 1981

Frans Jozef van Beeck, S.J.

CONTENTS

*There is a fundamental reason why sacramental theology
and practice must be renewed, namely, the breakdown of
conventional Christianity. Social change demands a new
style, just as it was social change that determined, at
least partly, the shape and the tone of traditional
practice and theology. Phenomena such as ritualism,
core-isolation, symbol-diminishment, reductionism in
theology and sacramental tutiorism and minimalism must
be criticized in the light of a more adequate notion of
validity, a new look at the function of church order,
and especially the new climate in ecclesiology as well
as the new self-awareness of the laity.*

*If we discount Baptism, the entire discussion of the
sacraments in ecumenical settings tends to be mired in
matters regarding validity. A new and free discussion
of this issue, therefore, is appropriate. It must insist on the marginal nature of validity in the ordinary course of sacramental events, and as a result, it
must insist on the fact that sacraments which are
technically invalid can be, and have been, interpreted
rather more liberally of late.*

Contents

THREE: CHURCH AND CHURCH DOCTRINE   57

*Sacraments are intimately connected with the unity of
the Church. Modern ecclesiology has tended far more
towards an eschatological orientation, so that the unity of the Roman Catholic Church has come to be viewed
as a relative one. At the same time, the ecclesial reality of the churches of the Reformation has been recognized — thus creating room for true sacraments in
these churches. In parallel fashion, sacramental doctrine is now viewed as far less absolute and more provisional, thus creating room for true sacraments even
in places where the traditional doctrines are rejected.*

FOUR: SACRAMENTS AND MINISTRY   75

*Sacraments have traditionally been linked with valid
orders. Still, a survey of the Roman Catholic tradition in this regard reveals a flexibility far greater
than has traditionally been assumed. Canon Law turns
out never to have been the ultimate determinant, but
rather the ecclesial situation, which at times was
not only "extraordinary" but even downright "paradoxical". This opens the possibility for Protestant
sacraments to be recognized as true sacraments. This
opens the issue of the established ministries in the
Protestant churches. The cardinal distinction between
the essence of the sacrament of Order and its canonical shape, and a fundamental discussion of the relationship between the church-community and the ordained
ministry lead to some surprising, albeit tentative,
conclusions.*

viii

FIVE: INTERCOMMUNION: A NOTE ON NORMS   125

*There is room already for communicatio in sacris,
and the question arises as to the norms governing
it. Norms derived from creeds and church orders are
valid and wholesome, but in practice they invariably
fall short of experienced needs. Trying to discuss
and solve the issue in terms of the dilemma "sign of
unity" versus "cause of unity" leads to a deadlock.
The discussion of the problem in terms of "shared
concerns" — a theme already discussed in the first
chapter — is far more profitable, and it throws an
important light on the ecclesiastical responsibility
of individual ministers of sacraments.*

ABBREVIATIONS

Dz   H. Denzinger, *Enchiridion Symbolorum Defi-nitionum et Declarationum de Rebus Fidei et Morum*, Editions up to the 31st (various revisions, by C. Bann-wart, J. B. Umberg, and K. Rahner), 1854-1957.

DS   H. Denzinger — A. Schönmetzer, *Enchiridion Symbolorum Definitionum et Declarationum de Rebus Fidei et Morum*, Editions from the 32nd (1963) onward.

Kirch   C. Kirch, *Enchiridion Fontium Historiae Ecclesiasticae Antiquae*, 6th Edition, 1947.

INTRODUCTION

B OOKS HAVE their ups and downs — *habent sua fata libelli*, so an obscure commentator on Horace's works, Terentianus Maurus, wrote around the end of the second century. Finished in 1970, with a British publisher's contract signed, sealed and delivered in the same year, this book was one of the many minor fruits of the ecclesiological and ecumenical heyday of the middle and late 'sixties. Three and a half years after it was finished the climate had changed considerably, and the publisher (whose output was now evincing a marked interest in mildly *avant-garde* social and international justice issues) returned the manuscript unpublished, having disregarded several letters of inquiry sent to him by the author, some of them testier than others, and all of them tending, somewhat unfashionably, toward the Defence of Contractual Justice.

Meanwhile, the climate has changed once more. I am teaching general sacramental theology again — yes, an *aggiornamento* version of the old *de sacramentis in genere!* — and the text of *Grounded in Love* has served me for quite a few years now to introduce a *fundamentally* ecumenical dimension into the discussion. It is this development, besides the encouragement of some good friends, which has led me to the present comeback, after an interval of eleven years, a spell long enough to have consigned treatises weightier than the present one to oblivion for good.

The word "fundamentally" was emphasized for a reason just now. The practical, slow-progress oriented, friendly though somewhat tame atmosphere of these past ten or fifteen years has favored many inter-church conversations as well as some pretty impressive if provisional statements of mutual agreement and growing consensus. Both the

Grounded in Love

preparation and the reception of these documents
have in turn generated a great deal of illuminating discussion. It looks as if many issues are
actually being hammered out; rough rocks are apparently being dressed and made to fit in place.
Could there really be a productive movement afoot
to build a new, unified communion of Christian
churches? Are these the new echoes of the old
church dedication hymn sung to celebrate Jerusalem
the heavenly city, the vision of peace — *caeles-
tis urbs Jerusalem, beata pacis visio* ?
    The hymn just mentioned is one sustained
song in praise of faithful craftmanship, of the
kind formerly associated with the comfortable in-
genuities of canon law and church order, and more
recently with ecumenical committee-work:

> *Scalpri salubris ictibus*
> *et tunsione plurima,*
> *fabri polita malleo,*
> *hanc saxa molem construunt,*
> *aptisque iuncta nexibus*
> *locantur in fastigio.* *

    Still, it is possible to be slightly too im-
pressed by snug fit and elegant structure. Then it
is time to recall that tall cathedrals stand erect
also because those medieval craftsmen succeeded in
reintegrating, at the basis, the quarried stones,
now dressed and shaped, with the live rock from
which they were first taken. If it is said of the
Church that she "stands tall, rising to the stars,
made of living stones" —

> *quae celsa de viventibus*
> *saxis ad astra tolleris* —

                                    this is so
only because the dressed stones and the tight
structures refer themselves back to the spiritual
Rock, the Church's one Foundation, Jesus Christ,

_____
*Through blows of wholesome chisel and much-repeated
beating, dressed down by craftsman's hammer, these rocks
mount to a building; snug joints hold them together, secure
in place on high.

present in the Spirit. The Church's height and
splendor are fully measured only as the awesome
depth of her foundation is fathomed.

The following five chapters have all this in
common that they try, *through the structures,* to
go back to the undressed, vital, living rock that
holds them up whether they realize it or not. In
theological terms, these chapters are concerned
with the exploration of basic ecclesial themes,
attitudes and orientations, and only in that sense
with the study of church order.

The modern city-dweller tends to take basic,
foundational facts for granted; the milk-bottle,
after all, is the rule and the cow the exception.
Similarly, loyal church-members, who generally enjoy the benefits of the structures or who at least
live with them, whether by circumstance or by de-
sign, are liable to find the sight of naked rock
somewhat disconcerting. Still, it is at this
deeper, more hidden level of the live rock rather
than at the level of man-made structure that the
common foundation of all Christian churches, all
of them so different in the form as well as the
feel of their worship and fellowship practices,
remains to be discovered. And once discovered,
the vitality, and indeed the charisma, of the basic presuppositions of ecclesiastical law and order will make their presence felt. For some this
will mean a sense of freedom; it may cause a sense
of frustration in others; in all, it is hoped, it
will create a sense of urgency. Why urgency? Because the unity of Christians is so deep and basic
a concern that it may never be sacrificed to the
comforts of ecclesiastical peace.

This applies, obviously, to the ecclesiastical and denominational establishments themselves;
ecumenism calls for flexibility, revision of confessional positions once taken, and willingness to
let unity arise where division used to be well established. (Pope John XXIII is said to have replied to a prelate who admitted he had concelebra-
ted the liturgy with an Orthodox bishop, with whom
he had also shared the Eucharist in the concentra-

3

tion-camp where they had met as fellow-priests, that the canon lawyers would lose their jobs if this kind of thing did not happen.) But it applies also to the very processes by which this unity is achieved and to the results to which these processes have led. Ecclesiastical people — clerical and lay — tend to overrate ecumenical achievements and to be gratified by the comforts they bring, rather than retain that holy restlessness that comes out of the Urge to worship the one and true God with groans too deep for words, and which will not settle for anything short of what Christ promised. Analogously, the study of theology tends — understandably — to concentrate on concrete and readily available advances in the ecumenical dialogue, rather than keep alive what has been called *la dialectique du provisoire* — the habit of turning good and hard-won answers into better and harder questions. Both the churches and the study of theology, therefore, stand to lose their souls if that *feu sacré*, which is the *agape* of Christ, does not keep the ground hot under their feet. No one but the Father can bring about the *eschaton*, but only those who have been indefatigable in trying to bring it on will recognize the sign of the Son of Man when he appears. It is this conviction which has determined the shape of this book, even more so now that it is finally published than when it was finished eleven years ago.

Essentially, all of the chapters in this book were published before. The first chapter first appeared in *Theological Studies* 30(1969)613-634. The original text of the next three chapters appeared in Dutch in *Bijdragen* 26(1965)129-179, and in English in the *Journal of Ecumenical Studies* 3 (1966)57-112; it was subsequently included in a collection of essays edited by my friend Nicholas Lash and entitled *Doctrinal Development and Christian Unity* (London, 1967; U.S. edition *Until He Comes*, Dayton, Ohio, 1968). The present version of these chapters owed a debt to remarks made by critics, notably George Tavard, in *Continuum* 6

(1968)260-269, and to volume 34 of *Concilium*. The
fifth and final chapter appeared, in article form,
in *One in Christ* 12(1976)124-141, when it looked
as if the manuscript of the completed book was never going to see the light of day.
   All of this implies that I have made no attempts at a bibliographical update. The main reason for this, apart from my own reluctance to re-
write the book completely, is the conviction stated in the previous paragraph: I wish to insist on
fundamental ecumenism. There are now numerous
subtle and impressive particular ecumenical advances in sacramental theology and practice, and they
are well documented and discussed as well as easily accessible in the pertinent sections of *Concilium*, the *Journal of Ecumenical Studies, The Ecumenist, Ecumenical Trends*, and the *Ecumenical Review*,
to mention only some familiar publications readily
available everywhere in the United States. This
availability of literature dealing with concrete
points, however, makes the scarcity of writings
dealing with basic questions all the more obvious,
and it is here, I fondly think, that *Grounded in
Love* may still make a difference.
   Not that I think that this book exhausts the fundamental issues. I wish to point to four themes
which I was pretty much unaware of ten or fifteen
years ago, and hence, which the present book does
not treat; yet is is obvious that they must be
part and parcel of any up-to-date sacramental theology conscious of its ecumenical task. They all
belong to the wider ecumenism that exceeds the
narrow bounds of the dialogue between Catholicism
and the Reformation, which was the setting of my
theological awakening.
   The broadest theme in modern sacramental theology must be *anthropology*: the human person must
be defined as *animal symbolicum*. The celebratory
enhancement of shared human life, experienced as
significant in an all-encompassing, life-giving
perspective, is something that characterizes human
kind as such. This realization should lead to a
basic, all-encompassing ecumenism in sacramental

theology. A unifying theme that comes to us mainly from the Orthodox world is the emphasis on *worship*; both Catholics and Protestants, in their eagerness to determine the nature of sacramental causality and signification, have tended to forget that sacraments are primarily celebrated in worship of the Father in and with and through Jesus Christ present in the Holy Spirit. This realization should put the divergent canonical and ecclesiastical aspects of sacramental theory and practice firmly in a common perspective.

Not only worship but also *witness* must become a basic unifying theme in sacramental theology. The living word that is joined to the element (to use St. Augustine's phrase) is neither purely authoritative or declarative, nor simply explanatory or commemorative, let alone magical; rather, it is what gives a sacrament its existential effectiveness. In the words of St. Thomas Aquinas, it is the *forma sacramenti*: it makes a sacrament what it is. Uttered in response to the living Christ present in the Spirit, it is heard in the Christian community as well as outside it as an urgent call to conversion and obedience of faith. To draw a bit closer to the Hebrew Bible, a sacrament is an *'ôt*: an act with a message, a gauntlet thrown down, a "ritualized prophetic memorial sign." As such, it not only betokens the faith of those involved in it, but also functions as a divinely-inspired challenge offered to those who believe weakly or not at all. This realization, too, should help liberate sacramental theology out of any small-minded ecclesiastical ghettoes.

Lastly, emphasis on worship and witness as well as awareness of the whole wide world of human kind must lead to the recognition of the *Holy Spirit* as the vital force in all sacraments. This will help put all the "objective" elements (church order, validity, doctrine, ministerial competence, etc.) in their proper places, since the Holy Spirit both inspires *and* *exceeds* whatever happens in the way of structure, canon law and order in mat-

ters sacramental. Here if anywhere we will do well
to realize that it is one Spirit that must be allowed to animate as well as blow apart the great
variety of separated ministrations.

Anthropology, liturgical theology, Word-theo-
logy, pneumatology: four sources of a truly ecumenical sacramental theology. At the same time,
such a sacramental theology largely awaits creative efforts at *construction* — efforts that will
place the traditional and the customary in a broad
and challenging context, and thus eventually
change it. The aims and methods of the present
book are much more limited; they are attempts at
re-construction rather than construction. Start-
ing from the sacraments as the Roman Catholic tradition has handed them down to us, we proceed to
ask questions about the vital assumptions that un-
derlie the canons, the distinctions and the divi-
sions, in search of common ground at the level of
bedrock.

Let us change the metaphor. Humanity, worship, witness, Holy Spirit: thank God there's
plenty of healthy breeze swirling around the well-
kept separate Christian churches. But it takes
people on the inside to open the windows — trusty
stewards, and they'd better know where the old keys
are kept to unlock them.

7

ONE:

Sacraments, Church Order,
and Secular Responsibility

IF TODAY is a bad day for people in positions of authority, it is so, too, for the scholar, whether he happens to be a theologian or a professional expert in any other field. Professional expertise has become strangely unbelievable. It sometimes seems as if the assurance with which authorities ecclesiastical as well as civil make it known that there is no need to worry, since "we have the experts working on the problem," usually achieves the opposite of reassurance: very often, the popular and public response is a funny kind of irritated suspicion. And this feeling of irritation gets decidedly worse when people are more or less outspokenly reminded by the authorities that only the experts can safely discuss these particular problems, since "they have the training" and they "know the facts." The suspicion of a kind of giant alliance between knowledge and power, whose sole purpose it is to keep the common person uninformed, is a reality that can be observed every day, much to the distress of those authorities who are genuinely concerned to come up with the best possible answers, only to find themselves accused, directly or indirectly, of wheeling and dealing, paternalism, feudalism, and lack of democratic spirit.

Still, the experts had better face the facts. And the facts are: a communications explosion, an education explosion, and a freedom explosion. For the expert this means: the academic Valhalla has been forced open. Recognition is no longer proportioned to his academic and scholarly standing

9

among his fellow-experts, but to his ability, in
the terms of his discipline, to interpret creat-
ively what everybody is vaguely aware of as happening in society, or in the Church, as the case
may be. Never much at home in the role of the lu-
natic, the lover, and the poet, today's scholar
will often painfully realize that the absence of
the prophet's mantle around his drooping shoulders
is only barely excused by people who have no idea
of the painstaking efforts involved in the slow
process of research. Yet the demand is there: by
popular vote the scholar is no longer allowed to
operate and express himself just on his own terms
and in his own terminology. All forms of authority and expertise are to an increasing extent being
based on the ability to empathize with society in
all its stratifications. Power of interpretation,
articulation and hermeneutic with regard to the
past and the present (if not the future) — in
other words: power of mass communication — has
become the condition of acceptance of all kinds of
authority, by Church and society alike.

Necessary background: social, "secular" change

The twin expression "Church and society" has not
been without purpose thus far. Any discussion of
church order is precarious in the sense that today
perhaps more than ever it is liable to degenerate
into a kind of ecclesiastical self-gratification.
There seems to be a certain psychosomatic connection between nearsightedness and paranoia, and
there is no reason to believe that the churches,
with their traditional suspiciousness with regard
to what is happening in the world, should miracul-
ously escape nearsightedness, mistaking intra-
church renewal for the most powerful perspective
available in today's world. If it is not understood that adaptation, updating, *aggiornamento* and
promotion of freedom must be a service of the
Church to the *world*, and not in the first place a
service of the Church to herself, then we run the
risk, in the words of bishop Robinson, of a "pre-

mature closing of the ecclesiastical ranks at the
cost of maintaining or widening the gulf between
the church and the world." [1] Going back to the
vivid language of the patristic period or even to
Scripture, more flexibility in canonical matters
(*epikeia*), endeavors to draft reunion-*symbola* and
exploring the forms and possibilities of intercommunion, experiments to arrive at liturgies that
convey meaning, curial reform both in Rome and at
the diocesan level, revision of administrative and
judicial procedures, revision of canon law — in
short, every form of concern with church order and
church doctrine, with "Faith and Order," runs the
risk of suffering from fundamental shortsighted-
ness, fear and suspiciousness. In other words: it
runs the risk of failing in faith and hope. For the
fact of the matter is that there *is* a connection
between the opening of the closed church-windows
and the heightened civic and social awareness of
millions of citizens inside and outside the Church.
All these people insist on perceiving in, or de-
manding from, church structures whatever they per-
ceive in, or demand from, secular society in the
way of goodness, justice, wisdom, freedom and humanity. If at the time of the first Vatican Council the Church was challenged to take account of
the aspirations of a very thin, rationally developed upper layer in society, which forced her to
articulate the reasonableness of faith and the coherence of ecclesiastical structures of belief and
governance, today she stands exposed in the middle
of a democratic, cosmopolitan world of free citizens, or at least citizens who consider themselves
on the way to freedom. This means that the challenge has become: to articulate and convey the relevance of the message of salvation to the world.
A new conception of church order, therefore, must
take cognizance of what is happening in the Secular City. It may not succumb to the temptation of
taking the way of least resistance, and refine the
church order only within the narrow framework of

1. David L. Edwards (ed.), *The Honest to God Debate*, S.
C. M. Press, Ltd., London, 1963, p. 250, n. 3.

intra-ecclesiastical assumptions, which are no
longer understood, let alone considered saving, by
people who are aware of the developments of society.

Tendencies in classical sacramental theology [2]

All sacraments except Baptism are hedged in by a
network of provisions regarding validity. That
Baptism has remained such a simple proposition is
probably due to the fact that the big questions
regarding Baptism had been asked and answered in
the controversy between Pope Stephen and Bishop
Cyprian in the middle of the third century, and in
Augustine's debates with the Donatists around the
year 400 A.D. — in other words, long before the
body of canon law as we know it began to develop.
As a result, the validity of Baptism, with the exception of the Arian controversy in the West and a
few marginal cases involving isolated sects, has
never been a real problem either theologically or
even at the level of church order. The recent ab-
olition of cautionary (*ad cautelam*) conditional
baptism in the case of a Christian first joining
the Roman Catholic Church is, therefore, of little
theological interest, no matter how many emotional
and administrative barriers had to be overcome on
this score. [3]

---

    2. After what has just been said it may seem incongru-
ous that this chapter sets out to treat the problem of church
order by means of a treatment of aspects of sacramental theology and practice. Yet this is not very strange; taken at
their "lowest" level, sacraments *are* juridical acts: participation in them shows that a person is a church-member in
good standing. Only the juridical level is not the most
typically sacramental aspect, let alone the only one! Cf.
P. Smulders, "Sacramenten en Kerk," *Bijdragen* 18(1956)391-
418; summary in French: "Sacrements et Eglise — Droit-Culte
-Pneuma," 418.
    3. Cf. DS 3874. In view of this sharing of Baptism,
stressed again by the Decree on Ecumenism of Vatican II, n.
22, it may be asked, not only whether conditional baptism
should be abolished, but also whether it would not be desir-

The other sacraments, however, are in quite a different position. The question that needs asking is the following: What made it possible for the sacraments to get encrusted by so many canonical provisions regarding validity and liceity? In what way did it become possible, for instance, for Confirmation to be valid only if administered by a bishop, at least in the Latin-rite church, except in cases provided for by canon 782, §2 of the Code of Canon Law as reinterpreted by later instructions? What are the key ideas behind the provisions regarding the Eucharist and its ministers, regarding faculties to absolve in Confession, regarding matrimonial canon law, especially the invalidating impediments? How has it been possible for the church order as expressed in canon law to arrive at such meticulous definitions of the minimal requirements for valid sacraments? In what way has church order succeeded in getting such a tight grip on those rites which, after all, are traditionally called "means of *grace*"?

It has been fashionable lately to blame canon law for this development. It would appear that this is a bit unfair; any legal system, taken by itself, tends to refine its definitions, to take care of the need for legal security. It is true, it was precisely this need for refined definition and security that led to such a high degree of ossification in sacramental church order, with the result that many Christians today fail to see or experience what kind of saving significance the sacraments are supposed to have. It appears, therefore, that *sacramental theology itself* must be held responsible for the tight hold which the canonical church order has managed to gain on the sacraments. Canon law would not have succeeded in doing this if the road to it had not been leveled by theology itself.

In this context three typical features of

---

able to change the rules that still determine in what denominational or ecclesiastical setting Baptism must be received. In other words, there is something to be said for claiming that Christians are baptized in *the* Church, not in *a* church.

classical sacramental theology deserve to be mentioned, namely, the tendency toward core-isolation
and symbol-diminishment, the tendency to reduction
as a method in theology, and tutiorism and minimalism in sacramental practice.

  1. *Ritualism, core-isolation, and symbol-diminishment.* It is, of course, unthinkable that in
the apostolic Church's awareness the celebrations
which we now call the seven sacraments were already isolated rituals. It has indeed been pointed out by studies like Oscar Cullmann's *Les sacrements dans l'évangile johannique* [4] that there
are a number of passages in the fourth Gospel with
clear eucharistic and baptismal overtones; others
have pointed to marriage symbolism in the same
Gospel, especially in the words of Jesus on the
cross, addressed to his mother and the beloved di-
sciple. These observations, however, are not meant
to convey the impression that any sort of entirely
defined and fully ritualized baptismal or eucharistic or matrimonial celebrations should have oc-
casioned the dialogues between Jesus and Nicode-
mus, the Samaritan woman, the disciples, and Mary.
The same point may be made about the accounts of
Jesus' meeting with the disciples on the road to
Emmaus in Luke, and about the accounts of the mul-
tiplication of loaves in all Gospels: if these
pericopes were short stories derived from ritually
isolated eucharistic celebrations, how to account
for the fact that the wine symbolism is lacking,
whereas the latter is present in the account of
Jesus' first sign at Cana and in the catechesis in
Hebrews, but without any reference to the bread?
Hence, we are to consider these pericopes (as well
as numerous others) as reflections of the vital
atmosphere of the community life of the first few
generations of Christians, when tradition and experience, authority and creative talent, liturgy
and life, order and charisma were hardly distinguished, let alone separated. A clear suggestion
in this direction is contained in the close rela-

---

  4. Subtitle: *La vie de Jésus et le culte de l'église
primitive*, P. U. F., Paris, 1951.

tionship between the formulas found in the Gospels
to express the power to forgive sins communicated
to the Twelve and those conveying the commission
to *all* Christians to forgive each other. The existence of a separate, isolated sacrament of Penance would seem to be excluded by these literary
data. [5]

As early as the first half of the second century, represented by writings such as the *Didache*,
the Letters of St. Ignatius of Antioch, and Justin
Martyr's first Apology, we can discern a clear delimitation of Baptism, the Eucharist, Holy Orders,
and even to an extent Marriage. [6] And a few
generations later, toward the end of the second
century, Hippolytus' *Traditio Apostolica* presents
us with a picture of clearly ritualized Roman cer-
emonials for Baptism, the Eucharist, and Holy Orders. [7] Thus a slow process of definition and

---

5. It would be possible, although not feasible here, to
multiply the examples. For the Eucharist the reader may be
referred to, *e.g.*, Johannes Betz, *Die Eucharistie in der
Zeit der griechischen Väter*, Bd. II/I, *Die Realpräsenz des
Leibes und Blutes Jesu im Abendmahl nach dem neuen Testament*, Freiburg, 1961.

6. No matter how floating the type of Church represented by the *Didache*, there is a distinct concern with order:
this is borne out by the distinction between the true prophet and the false (11, 3-12), the rules for Baptism, even
with a beginning of casuistry (7, 1-4), and the rules for
the Eucharist (9, 1 - 10, 6), with, characteristically, leeway to the prophets (10, 7). — The specificity of the sacraments in the writings of Ignatius is, of course, immediately related to the fact that in the community nothing can be
done without the bishop, as Ignatius insists in numerous
passages. Thus the bishop and those authorized by him are
the presiding officers at the eucharistic celebrations (*e.g.
Phil.* 4; 8), and marriages are entered upon in the presence
of the bishop (*Polyc.* 5). — For Baptism in Justin Martyr's
first Apology, cf. ch. 61; for the Eucharist on Sundays, cf.
ch. 65-67.

7. Consecration of bishops: 2-3; eucharistic prayer: 4;
ordination of presbyters: 8; ordination of deacons: 9; Baptism: 20-23.

Grounded in Love

delimitation can be observed, which was to find its
culmination in the scholastic doctrine of sacramental matter and form, which led to a final definition of the sacraments. [8] How tortuous the road
could be is shown by the development of the sacrament of Penance: the forgiveness of sins, preached
by Jesus as a condition for the gift of the Father's mercy, and communicated by him to the
Twelve, moves, via the spiritual direction given
by the charismatic monks in the East, the Western
canonical penance and epsicopal *exomologesis*, the
deathbed confession of Isidore of Seville and the
tariffed confessions of the Irish monks, to the
auricular confession of the high Middle Ages and
Trent: isolated, ritualized, delimited.

It is only natural that this ritual isolation
of the sacraments had its influence on the shape
of their liturgical celebration; once the sacraments had drifted apart from the rest of Christian
life, their celebration had to be emphatically

---

8. The end of this tradition is hopefully marked by Pius XII's definition of the matter and form of the sacrament
of Order in 1947 (DS 3857-3861). — The decree of the Holy
Office of 1957 regarding the rite of concelebration (DS 3928)
is nothing but an application of a long-standing norm, although its enforcement here is quite ruthless and dogmatic-
ally overstated. The decree insufficiently acknowledges the
collegial nature of any type of concelebration, and it sins
by overdefinition ("in virtue of Christ's institution only
he validly consecrates who pronounces the words of consecration.") The latter becomes even more unbelievable if it is
remembered that some pre-Nicene eucharistic rites may not
even have contained the institution narrative. According to
Gregory Dix (*The Shape of the Liturgy*, Dacre Press, Westmin-
ster, 1945, pp. 239-240), the use of our Lord's words of institution as "consecratory" came to be accepted slowly by
the Church, according as they were felt to be the prime articulation of what the community was actually *doing* in the
Eucharist. At one time it must have been felt sufficient if
the rite was performed after the manner of the Last Supper.
The precise verbalization of the "consecration" was a process of "drawing out and expounding" meaning, not of meaning
being "added to" an essentially meaningless rite.

something special. Questions began to be asked a-
bout the real essence, not of *agape* or the forgiveness of sins, but of the Eucharist and Confession.
The minimal shape of the sacraments was eventually
laid down, and with that, the sign was gradually
"clarified" and "purified" of all that was too ordinary, too humdrum, too crude. The sacrament in
its "purest" form arose: the ritual gesture of
anointing, the immaculately white wafer, the quiet
hand that gives absolution with a formalized formula whispered in the ear. [9]

This somewhat tendentious survey of a factual
development does not mean to be a plea in favor of
a return to the primitive Church. Ritualization,
refinement and stylistic emphasis are the normal
products of the development of symbolic activity.
The fact that the sacraments, especially Baptism
and the Eucharist, began to be somewhat dissoci-
ated from the rest of Christian life within the
first half century after the death and resurrection of Jesus contributed much to the exploration
and the depth of the Christian faith, for that is
what sacraments were from the beginning: a vital,

---

9. It is tempting at this point to write a whole chapter about the ambiguities and crises fostered by the style
in which the sacraments are celebrated today. A few rough
outlines may suffice to convey the present writer's opinions in this regard. — Because of the emphatic, non-pract-
ical and in that sense abstract, formal nature of the symbol, a certain amount of ambiguity is inherent in sacramental celebrations as such, since they have to move in that narrow area where the precarious balance between evocative quality
and expressiveness on the one hand, and stylization on the
other hand is maintained. Overemphasis on the former (*e.g.*
in the interest of "relevance") may prevent the celebration
from reaching out beyond what is heard and seen; overemphasis on the latter may turn it into magic. The history of
the liturgy provides instances of both, but the bane of a
lot of official present-day liturgy is mostly the latter.
And if people then stay away from the sacraments, the correct diagnosis is not, "The people don't believe in the
Mass any more," but rather, "The Mass does not seem to lead
the people to believe in the *invisibilia* any more."

creative catechesis, a habitual introduction of the
faithful to the depths and demands of the Christian way of life.

But it is also true that a real danger gradually became a fact as a result of this relative i-
solation. The sacramental nature of Christian
life as a whole was lost sight of: *this* was a sacrament and *that* wasn't, and within the celebration
called a sacrament *this* was essential and *that* was
not. But clear-cut distinctions like these give,
of course, a large scope to the development of a
legal system, which will then set itself the task
of elaborating with the help of casuistry when and
on what conditions a rite can, or cannot, be a
sacrament.

2. *Reduction as a method in theology.* A second handle offered to canon law by traditional
sacramental theology is what may be called reduction as a method in theology. By this is meant
the apparently ineradicable tendency in Latin theology to moor everything that lives and moves to
an anchor at the level of substance, in which is
then located the essential core of the sacrament.

This tendency towards reduction shows up, not
only in sacramental theology, but also in several
other areas. Thus, the traditional doctrine of
the *inclusio* of all of human kind in the humanity
of Jesus Christ [10] is a typical example of the
reduction of salvation to the level of the hypo-
static, ontological structure of the God-Man. The
reasoning is as follows. Whoever is saved is saved
in Christ; this is antecedently true for all of
human kind, and thus all of human kind must have
been included, prior to everything, in the God-Man,
otherwise redemption for all of human kind would
have been impossible, since "what has not been assumed has not been healed." [11] Similar reduc-

10. For a full and competent discussion of this doctrine the reader is referred to F. Malmberg, *Ein Leib, ein
Geist*, Freiburg, 1960, pp. 223-273.

11. Gregory Nazianzen's famous phrase in his letter to
Cledonius; cf. J. N. D. Kelly, *Early Christian Doctrines*,
Revised Ed., San Francisco, 1978, pp. 296-297. For the the-

tions have led to all too strongly hypostaticized
notions about, *e.g.*, original sin and the substan-
tial presence of Christ in the Eucharist. [*12*] But
the real question is whether this reduction to sub-
stantiality is as necessary for disciplined, "objective" theological thinking as has often been
maintained, and indeed whether it is not just one
out of many very particular thinking patterns —
which would mean that it has no more authority
than any other methodological model. [*13*]

---

ory that the doctrine of *inclusio* must be understood as a
rhetorical device, meant to convey a relational, not a sub-
stantial point (*viz.* that nothing human is alien to Christ,
and that therefore all human concerns are accepted and included in him, cf. my *Christ Proclaimed — Christology as Rhetoric*, New York - Ramsey - Toronto, 1979, pp. 154-162, 360-
385, 510, 566-573.

    12. It is not without reason that a theologian like P.
Schoonenberg has done some of his most significant work precisely on these points, with the intention of *relating* original sin and transubstantiation again to the total reality
of sin and the Eucharist respectively. The fact that a by-
gone age could afford to conceive of "realities" mainly in
terms of hypostaticized entities is no reason why our era
should not attempt a new approach, in which the notion of relationship would play an extremely important part.

    13. This problem involves, of course, the question of
hermeneutics. I for one have a hunch that such doctrines as
the inclusion of human kind in the humanity of Jesus, the
indelible character conveyed by some sacraments, the reality
of original sin, and other similar "objective," hypostaticized notions, even in their most formal hellenistic-scholas-
tic attire, were a lot more "existential," "related," "symbolic," and even "metaphorical" in their heyday than we are
inclined to believe, or even capable of believing. It was
said of Thomas Aquinas that he was in the habit of speaking
very terminologically — *frater Thomas formalissime loquitur* — , but that need not mean that his ability to work
with clear, well-defined concepts implied that he was unaware of the existential relationships between the realities
so very formally defined. I would not be in the least surprised if the present-day need for a new theological language (which I endorse) were not to a large extent caused by

Grounded in Love

An example from sacramental theology. In the Donatist controversy Augustine resisted the idea of Catholic reordination of clergy who had been ordained by Donatist bishops, or who had served in the Donatist church for a while, just as he also resisted the idea of a second Baptism for those baptized by Donatist clergy. If it is Christ who justifies, Christ who seals, Christ who acts through the sacramental ministry, how can anyone interfere and repeat Baptism or Ordination? Latin theology was to interpret this Augustinian doctrine in terms which remind one of substance and accident: if ordination to the ministry cannot be repeated, then there must be an enduring reality at the level of "soul" or "substance" [*14*] in spite of all "superficial" changes. Sacramental practice, and its interpretation in terms of relatedness to Christ and the Church are thus reduced to some-

---

the rise of the scientific world-view, to the process of dissociation of sensibility in Western civilization (T. S. Eliot), to the relatively recently acquired habit of isolating, objectifying observation, analysis and definition. Thomas Aquinas, after all, (unlike the neo-scholastics!) lived in an age in which the physical world, from which speculative thought borrowed most of its metaphors, was still a vital environment rather than a collection of objects. Incomprehensible though it may seem, even Kant's critical questions had not been asked. To blame our speculative impasse entirely on the "hellenization of dogma" seems to me a bit too pat to be true, unless one were to endorse Heidegger's view that the *entire* tradition of inauthentic thought goes back to the hypostaticizing, thing-ifying conceptualization tendencies which lie at the basis of Western culture. But even there I hesitate. Does our tendency to analyze, formalize and objectify not go back to the (Phoenician?) invention of alphabetic spelling? Still, whatever the causes of our impasse may be, I agree with Dewart *et al.* give up on "metaphysical" theological conceptualizations in favor of a more vital, synthetic, "ontic" articulation of the experience of faith.

14. There is no doubt that in Augustine's theology the so-called indelible *character* still enjoys the full, relational meaning of "relationship to Christ and the Church."

20

thing objective, apparently inert, *en soi*, and ontological, namely, the indelible character, which is then further identified — and here the reduction becomes really dangerous — as the *sacramentum et res*. The next step is obvious: the objectified character is in its turn used as a premiss, for instance by arguing that, since the sacrament of Order confers this character, someone who has been once ordained *cannot* be reordained, because he is a priest in eternity [15] quite apart from the question whether it will ever occur to him to leave the ministry for a while or for good. To sum up: a living, functional sacramental practice has been reduced to an objective and ontological prerequisite, which is then subsequently described as the *essence* of the sacrament; in this way, the sacrament is placed, as the expression goes, *in indivisibili* — you either have it or you don't. Once this has occurred it is up to the canon lawyers' ingenuity to decide with juridical impartiality when and on what conditions a sacrament is valid or invalid.

3. *Sacramental tutiorism and minimalism.* The two characteristics already mentioned naturally lead to a third trend to be briefly discussed, namely, the connection between tutiorism and minimalism in matters sacramental — both of them important tendencies in Roman Catholic sacramental discipline since late scholasticism.

A strongly isolated celebration, whose essence is almost exclusively defined in objective, ontological terms (so often giving the impression that sacramental grace is a possession rather than a gift, as the Reformation has not tired of pointing out to the Catholic tradition) is incapable of being treated with flexibility (*epikeia*, or, as

---

15. An interesting misapprehension. The fact that sacraments are part of the Church's pilgrim state, its *status viae*, is overlooked, with the result that we are but one step away from regarding the priestly *character* as the eternal private property of the priest, who then goes on, almost accidentally, to put *his* priestly powers at the disposal of the faithful. Cf. below, p. 143, note 23.

21

the Greek Orthodox say, *oikonomia*), or to have probabilism applied to it. If the fixed essence of the sacrament is not actualized, then there is no sacrament; if it is, then there is a sacrament. There is no room for assumptions and probable opinions here, but only an absolute tutiorism: imminent danger of death is, according to many of the classical textbooks of moral theology, the only ground that can justify exposing a sacrament to the risk of vacuity.

But on the other hand it is also true that in a way no more is needed than the essence for a sacrament to be a sacrament. Traditional theology knows, of course, the difference between a merely valid sacrament and a fruitful sacrament. Still, the overriding impression is very often that classical theology views fruitfulness as not a part of the sacrament. The minimal sacrament being the real cause, all that remains to be said of the fruit of the sacrament is that it is the effect — one that is indeed required for salvation, but still essentially accidental. Thus in many older catechisms the minimal conditions for a valid Confession were enumerated, especially with regard to the sufficiency of imperfect contrition or "attrition", whereas even Thomas Aquinas had taught (clearly assuming that contrition is the normal state of a penitent) that there can be no justification of a sinner without love of God and a penitential rejection of sin. [16]

Sacramental minimalism on the one hand and tutiorism on the other: these two have resulted in a dangerous tendency to equate the maximal and the minimal status of the sacraments, in complete opposition to all human and Christian experience and tradition. A very clear example is Marriage. Ac-

----

16. Cf. I–II, q. 112, a. 2; q. 113, a. 3. With regard to the minimalistic approach to the sacrament of Penance, one is reminded of Pascal's outcry, in the tenth letter of the *Provinciales*: *Le prix du sang de Jésus-Christ sera de nous obtenir la dispense de l'aimer.* ("We were bought by the blood of Jesus Christ, and now it will buy us the dispensation from loving him.")

cording to the current provisions of Canon Law the
marriage service witnessed by an authorized priest
plus the physical consummation constitute the sacrament. It would seem that these are pretty minimal conditions for a sacrament, but the church
order does not seem to be aware of any other conditions for a Christian marriage. At the same
time, an almost absolute tutiorism is practised on
these very points, both with regard to the cerem-
ony and the consummation; it is not just a theor-
etical possibility that the reality of the sacrament has to be established in the land registry
office (where the parish boundaries are kept) or
under the microscope (where the issue of impotence
may have to be decided). In any case it must be
said that Canon Law has acquired a disproportion-
ate hold over the sacraments, once their natures
had become hardened and objectified in this fashion. Recent practice in the Roman Catholic marriage courts has, thank God, accepted a much wider range of causes for annulment.

     The three tendencies discussed so far pre-
sent, of course, a very incomplete picture, to
which a lot of further background should really
be supplied. One of the principal background
phenomena is the fact that with the rise of the
popular church, after the year 313 A.D., and to a
still larger extent after the conversion of the
Germanic tribes, a very profound change in sacramental sensibility set in. The Christian sacraments and the Christian feasts gradually took o-
ver the function of the pagan festivals. They
became, not so much the cultic interpretations
and actualizations of a deeply rooted Christian
faith, as the *means* of grace for the benefit of
semi-pagan church-members, whose conversion was
mainly associated with politico-feudal motives,
and in any case consisted of little more than the
sign of the Cross, the Our Father, the Hail Mary,
and the profession of the One God in Three Persons, the Incarnation and Death of God the Son,
and the promise of divine reward and punishment.
This led to an increasing clericalization of sac-

23

ramental practice — a phenomenon vigorously pro-
tested against by the Albigensians and the Waldensians in the early Middle Ages. Still, the
development went on; the clergy, wrongly appeal-
ing to Paul's phrase "stewards of God's mysteries"
(1 Cor 4, 1), became the body of the initiated,
who from time to time put the mysteries at the
disposal of the masses, too. No wonder that under
these circumstances sacramental symbolism more and
more became the over-refined liturgical etiquette
of a professional elite isolated from the body of
the faithful. Finally, to mention one more fact,
sacramental theology was deeply influenced by the
individualization of the "use" of the sacraments
(*usus sacramentorum*). Sacraments got isolated; so
did individual Christians. The key issue is no
longer the Church as the community of the faithful, but the salvation of one's own soul. [*17*]

Sacraments and church order: towards a new relationship

It seemed illuminating to survey some aspects of
the past history of the sacraments at some length,
because it is difficult to develop a fresh conception of church order without going to the root
of the present connection — or lack thereof —
between church order and sacramental life. A new-
style church order could not possibly content itself with a mere adaptation of the existing type
of Canon Law. In the light, not only of recent

---

17. I have sometimes wondered whether it would not be
possible to show a connection between the factors enumerated
in these last few lines. I for one would not be surprised
if there were a real psychological coherence in the pattern
comprising facts like the following: the officially celibate
clergy of the early Middle Ages; the development of the
highly refined, elaborate rubrical etiquette in the (mostly
private) Mass; such expressions as *hostia immaculata* used to
refer to the pure, white, thin wafer; the restriction of the
notion "Church" to the (literate) clergy; the countless *apo-
logiae* protesting the priest's impurity in the liturgy of the
Mass, with their strong emphasis on the need for forgiveness, and other similar phenomena. Compulsive tendencies?

social developments [*18*], but also of recent ecclesiology and sacramental theology, we must say
that the very foundations and assumptions of current Canon Law are no longer verified. This, of
course, does not mean that any type of church order or Canon Law will henceforth be a thing of the
past; the fact that there has been such a thing as
church order from the very beginning of Christianity, witness, *e.g.*, 1 Corinthians and Matthew, is
enough warrant that there will be church order in
the future, too. But church order must not be i-
dentified with any given historical form of church
order; it can adopt new orientations as radically
different as times and cultures may differ from
one another.

In the present context it would seem to be
profitable to consider three aspects of what could
possibly become the new-style church order: the
notion of validity, the essential function of
church order, and the relationship between the
Church and the modern world.

1. *The notion of validity.* "Valid" originally
means "powerful." In that sense something is valid when the power, the creativity, the strength of
life shows itself in it. This holds true for the
sacraments, too: they are valid according as the

---

18. The insights of Harvey Cox and others have helped
to articulate some of these developments. Let us make only
one point here. For the citizen of modern rational *Gesellschaft* (society) it is no use to pine for the return of the security of the kind of ready-made *Gemeinschaft* (community) of which
the village and the clan are the prototypes; the course of
Western civilization cannot be reversed. What *Gemeinschaft*
will be shaped in the future will have to be of persons' own
choosing, including the *communio sanctorum*. As the law-and-
order relationships of society are being continually challenged by the personal relationships of the large human fam-
ily in the making, so the Church as *Gesellschaft* will only
make sense if she does everything to meet the demand for
personal freedom. One is reminded in this context of Karl
Rahner's prophetic insights, thirty years ago, about the
Church *in diaspora*, and even further back, of Max Scheler's
Wesen und Formen der Sympathie.

the power of the redemption, the power of the
Kingdom breaks through in them. Seen within the
framework of the Church, the validity of a sacrament basically means: the recognition that a particular rite or ministry or state of life, in virtue of its inner relationship with Christ's institution in the past and his presence now, is an ef-
fectual sign and pledge of the Kingdom of God, the
new heaven and the new earth. [*19*]
    Recent sacramental theology prefers to call
sacraments "signs" or "symbols" rather than causes, and for a good reason: we must emphasize again
that sacraments make visible the faith and the
challenges implied in the Christian way of life.
Modern theology — and, it should be added, the
countless present-day liturgical experiments, those
above ground as much as those underground — have
precisely this in common, that they are attempting
to bridge the gaps which traditional sacramental
doctrine and practice had left: the gaps between
sacraments and life (the isolating tendencies),
between sacraments and the faithful seen as individual persons (the overemphasis on the ontological, objective aspects of the sacraments, or, as
the Reformation might put it, the practice of sacraments as "data of nature"), and among the faithful themselves (the absence of community dimension
leading to individualization). A sacrament is a
meaningful gesture, sign exchanged among living
beings (*signum datum inter viventia*), as Saint Augustine expressed it. Participation in a sacrament, therefore, always implies an option, a
choice, a free acceptance of the grace [*20*] as well
as the evangelical mission implied in the gift of
grace. This means that a sacrament is essentially
an existential gesture of a free person. This

19. For a further discussion of validity, cf. below,
chapter II, pp. 41ff..
    20. Note Trent's emphasis on freedom in its account of
the process of justification: "... by the free acceptance of
the grace and the gifts" (*per voluntariam susceptionem gra-
tiae et donorum* — DS 1528); cf. also: "they freely move toward God" (*libere moventur in Deum* — DS 1526).

liberty, this freedom of choice is part of the essence of the sacrament and will therefore have to be respected by the church order. This has consequences for the evaluation of the validity of those sacraments which are, or were, administered without an adequate choice on the part of the recipient. If and when at a later date the recipient would be morally incapable of recognizing the option implied in the sacrament as truly his own option, the church order should not view the fact that he or she has actually received the sacrament as a simple data of nature, a bare fact of history which it is now the person's destiny to be forever saddled with. One thing that follows from this that the canonical status of the *ab acatholicis nati* (baptized children of totally non-practising parents) is in dire need of revision, as is the situation of all sorts of other baptized and ordained and married Catholics (and other Christians) who withdraw from the Christian scene for a while and later return to it. [*21*]

The realization that a sacrament implies an option leads to a second point, namely, that there is a difference between church order and civil order — an issue to be further explored here.

2. *The function of church order.* When Paul, especially in his first letter to the Corinthians, describes the function of church order in the context of "knowledge" (*gnosis*) and "love" (*agape*), this is his *leitmotiv*: the Christian has been set free from the slavery of the Law, but he must not use this liberty as a pretext for self-will and self-love. This is the fundamental law that determines all church order. Its functioning is predicated on free choice: no one has a duty to be

---

21. In 1948 Pius XII ruled that non-Catholic marriages of *ab acatholicis nati*, which the Code of Canon Law had considered valid, were henceforth invalid. The new rule may have been cleaner and juridically more consistent; it was hardly calculated to do justice to reality, since it failed to take into account that a Baptism in no way endorsed by later Christian practice simply cannot be taken to imply any choice at all.

in the Church, but if someone does choose to be
in the Church, a binding appeal can be made for
such a person to abide by the church order for the
sake of *agape*.

This has far-reaching consequences. If it is
the free obedience of faith of those who respond
to the Gospel with a personal act of faith that
lies at the basis of the church order, then the
church order has no strictly objective claim to
human allegiance. In this regard there is an essential difference between church order and civil
order, since the latter holds good for every citizen, regardless of loyalty, which means that it is
far more objective. For even though in many cases
civil law successfully appeals to the good will
and the sense of responsibility of the individual
citizen, yet no sooner does the individual fail to
respond favorably than the law is enforced by means
of sanctions, in the interest of the public order
or the common good. [22]

Canon Law as we have it, however, especially
in relation to the sacraments of Baptism, Marriage,
Orders and (at least with regard to ecclesiastical
censures) Penance, betrays far too strongly its
civil origins. This is not to deny that the Church
rendered an enormous service to the world when she
jumped to the defense of civil order in the Dark
Ages, which were also the period that saw the origin and growth of the basic *corpora* of Canon Law.
Neither is this chapter the place to call in doubt

---

22. The distinction between church order and civil order here proposed tries to be a bit milder than the one proposed by John L. McKenzie in *Authority in the Church* (New
York, 1966), which takes a surprisingly dim view of authority in civil society and a disappointingly unrealistic view
of authority in the Church. Love and service (the latter of
which notions is distorted by the biased translation of *dia-
konos* — "servant" — by "lackey") are made to look a bit
too rosy to suit my taste. After all, excommunication *is* a
possibility in the New Testament, both in Matthew (18, 15-
18) and Paul (1 Cor 5). The question is only whether an ecclesiastical excommunication should be the response to a
purely objective transgression of a purely objective law.

the merits of the close ties between church order
and civil order in, *e.g.*, the Holy Roman Empire,
and in the sovereign states with their Established
Churches afterwards. So much is certain today
that the order of the Church in the midst of the
Secular City will unconditionally have to abandon
these close associations with the exercise of civil law, especially by resolutely disposing of any
kind of "automatic" jurisdiction, whereby people
come under church law without any participation on
their part. The civil order can afford, on certain occasions, to disregard the fact that the
justice and equity of a particular law are not appreciated by some citizens, and enforce it anyway.
The church order can hardly ever do this, since
its claim to obedience is never wholly objective.
This has a few consequences.

The first is that the church order *as such*
may not seek to keep people in the Church. When
in 1 Corinthians 5 Paul is treating the case of
the man who is living with his father's wife, he
orders the community to excommunicate this person,
but he concludes: "For what business is it of mine
to judge those outside? Do you not yourselves
judge those who are inside? And those who are
outside God will judge." In view of 1 Cor 4, 5
("Do not pronounce judgment before the time, before the Lord comes") this text must be understood
to uphold the validity of the church order without
its being wholly identified with God's judgment.
Church order is discipline, and as such it is the
concrete shape of mutual responsibility, care and
indeed *agape*. [23] But although love is in a very
real way a judgment of all that is against love,
[24] the judgment of the Church is provisional; it

---

23. C. K. Barrett (*The First Epistle to the Corinthians,*
Black, London, 1968, p. 132) rightly points out that Paul's
reaction is not one of censoriousness but of church discipline, nor does he "claim that he judges the church members."
It might be added, however, that Paul *does* act as an authoritative spokesman.

24. Cf. Paul Tillich's treatment of excommunication:
Systematic Theology, Chicago, 1967, III, pp. 179-180.

may never create the impression of finality, of
being tantamount to God's judgment. Church order
may never drive consciences into a tight corner;
if it does, people will stay in the Church out of
fear of damnation, and thus, in a spirit of slavery. [25] Neither may church order capitalize on
the lack of sophistication of the so-called simple
faithful in this regard.

This leads to the conclusion that leaving the
Church for reasons of failure, or refusal, to com-
ply with the church order must be presented as a
real and conscientious possibility; this would
seem to be a necessary corollary to the doctrine
of the gratuity of grace and the principle of the
liberty from the spirit of slavery. Church order
must be proposed in such a way that those who com-
ply with it do not arrive at the conclusion that
they have vested interests in the Church or a secure grip on salvation. The reverse side of this
proposition is that that same church order must be
so applied as to make it clear that free obedience
of faith is the only basis on which one can stay
in the Church or return to her. [26]

------

25. And that is *not* what Trent means when it realist-
ically but moderately says that it is not without profit for
the faithful to be shaken by the fear of God's justice (.. *a
divinae iustitiae timore ... utiliter concutiuntur* — DS
1526). There is a world of difference between the tyrannic-
al protectiveness of the Grand Inquisitor and the spiritual
realism ("realizing they are sinners": *peccatores se esse
intelligentes* — DS 1526) of the Decree on Justification.

26. If it is true, as I think it is, that *The End of
Conventional Christianity* (cf. the book by W. H. van de Pol,
Newman Press, New York, 1968) has come, it may well turn out
to be a paramount pastoral duty to teach people how to live
outside the visible Church and without the sacraments in
peace of mind and a good conscience. This does not mean
that the limits of the Church are going to be as clearly
marked in the future as they used to be in conventional
Christianity. On the contrary, if the relationship between
the Church and the world is really going to change, odds are
that a vital margin will develop as a traffic-area between
the Church as a visible society and the world.

A second consequence. If the church order
may not let itself be cajoled into keeping people
under tutelage, neither may it let itself be tempted to excommunicate them with a blessing. In other words, if it seemed just now that excommunication accompanied by a pointer to conscience and
God's mercy would be an easy way to enforce a
clear and general church order, we must now add
that precisely because church order is based on
free obedience of faith it must itself be pliant,
spacious, and trust-inspiring, and as much as possible. No matter how much scandal was given by
the eating of meat offered to idols, Paul does not
lay down an absolute law, although he does draw up
some rules as an expression of the community's responsibility for the consciences of the weaker
brethren, "for whom Christ died" (1 Cor 8, 11).
The church order, therefore, should also be such
as to give the faithful scope for, and to educate
them to, *personal* responsibilities *within* the
framework of the church order. [27] Would it not
be possible, *e.g.*, to have the nullity of a marriage established on the basis of conscientious statements, under oath, of the parties themselves?
Must the *favor iuris* (*i.e.* the assumption that a
marriage is taken to be valid unless the contrary
is proved) not be abolished? A marriage is, after
all, sacramental only if it is an enactment of the
unity of Christ and the Church, but it so happens
that this cannot be ascertained with absolute ob-
jectivity, given the fact that personal choices
and commitments can only be objectified to a limited extent.

This leads to a third consequence. If everything goes well, a legal order, and therefore also
the church order, does not function at all; the
point is that in most cases the provisions of
church order add nothing to the ordinary course of
events. [28] This means that a number of provis-

---

27. Thus we might see an end put to the situation which a
Dutch comedian summed up as follows: "In the Catholic Church everything is forbidden, except what's permitted, and that's a must."
28. This will be further explained below, pp. 46ff..

ions which are no longer practiced should be abolished. Let us enumerate a number of them. The
demand that infants should be baptized as soon as
possible after birth and the entire concept of eucharistic fast should be dropped. There should be
a major effort, before the sacrament of Penance
falls into complete disuse, to free it from all
the mechanistic associations it has acquired; this
would seem to mean that a form of truly communal
celebration of Penance should be introduced fast,
and with regard to private confession the practice
of granting faculties should be drastically sim-
plified and extended. The provisions with regard
to Sunday observance should be changed so as to
allow for personal choice, not only with regard to
time, but also with regard to the nature of the
celebration, which would not necessarily have to
be the Eucharist. With regard to the choice of
marriage-partner and the type of marriage-service
a large number of personal decisions have already
been generally practiced for quite some time; all
of this should be recognized, especially in the
case of mixed marriages, whose situation has been
changing so rapidly. In general, the liturgical
freedom that is being practiced both above ground
and underground should be recognized as generally
desirable and fruitful. Ordination of married
persons should be introduced. These and similar
changes would seem to be necessary to prevent the
church order from dropping behind the facts to
such an extent that contempt of law — *contemptus
legis* — would ensue.

3. *Church order and the fading margin.* [29]
The problem of church order, however, is not just
a problem of how to do justice to the need for
responsibility and freedom in the Church. It has
become increasingly clear over the past twenty or
thirty years that the issue must be raised in a
totally new way. As the clear distinctions between the (institutional) Church and the world
have become relative, and as the dynamic nature of

---

29. With a bow to my friend the late Francis X. Shea,
of Boston College, to whom I owe this expression.

faith in the mystery of Christ has been rediscovered, a number of what used to be marginal phenomena have become part of the regular life of the
Church. From the point of view of the prevailing
church order many of these "cases" can hardly, if
at all, be placed within the framework of the ecclesiastical institutions; yet in very many instances they are so obviously evangelical in inspiration and tone that it would be foolish — theologically! — to discount them or to write them off
as irrelevant to a renewed ecclesiology.

One of the most interesting and disturbing
features of the past few decades has been the development of a "marginal church" which claims for
itself loyalty to the inspiration without an equal
degree of loyalty to the institution. For those
who, in the wake of Pius XII's encyclical on the
Church as the Mystical Body (*Mystici Corporis*),[30]
deny the possibility of any opposition between the
institution and the inspiration, this margin is
bound to represent a direct onslaught on the unity
of the Church and its orthodoxy. In their eyes
the margin is not a margin but a fringe. They
plead for clear identity by means of clear definition and delimitation.

But the fact is that the marginal church is
not a fringe phenomenon, but one that penetrates
the whole Church, and for that matter, all Christian
Churches. It is found in the shape of the "third
man" described by François Roustang, [31] who is
neither the fully-committed, classical church-mem-

---

30. Cf. DS 3800-3822. H. Küng has noted that the new
edition of Denzinger, edited by Schönmetzer, omits the passage from the encyclical *Humani Generis* which in the old Dz
was included as nr. 2319, where Pius XII wholly identifies
the Mystical Body with the Roman Catholic Church (*Truthfulness: The Future of the Church*, New York, 1968, p. 154). The
Constitution on the Church of Vatican II, *Lumen Gentium*, § 8,
has the interesting expression "*subsistit in*", which replaces the "*est*" of the draft constitution; thus, the second Vatican Council teaches that the Church founded by Christ "has
actuality in" or "subsists in" the Roman Catholic Church.
31. *Christus* 13(1966)561-567.

ber nor the person who leaves the faith and the
Church, but the person who is no longer really in-
terested in creed and church order, who is irritated by the institution but lives with it pretty
much on his own terms, while all the time committed to staying in the Church in order to be inspired by the Gospel and to celebrate the sacraments.
The margin also occurs in radical and very often
highly experimental theologizing by very committed
Christians; in radical ecumenical experiments,
both in the form of joint outreach to the under-
privileged and in the form of joint sacramental
worship; in the liturgical and evangelical vent-
ures of the underground-church, basic-community
or floating-parish type; in the increasing number
of Christians — not just partners in mixed marriages — who consider themselves Christians with
close ties to more than one church. [32]

Let us take an example and analyze it a bit.
It represents a good illustration of the way the
church order can be faced with an impasse. There
have been, for at least fifteen years, scattered
instances of eucharistically-inspired *agape*-cele-
brations, recently also presided over by Catholic
women. The groups that have practiced them inva-

---

32. It would be unrealistic to suggest that all these
events and experiments are always and everywhere the fruit
of the purest Christian inspiration; but what, for that matter, is? There is no doubt a serious amount of reaction a-
gainst authority and structure in all of this, a fair amount
of freakishness and impatience, and — worst of all in my
view — a good deal of self-gratification, liturgical and
otherwise. Nevertheless, it seems necessary to make three
points. [1] It is always unwise to disregard a phenomenon
that is so widespread. [2] Not everything need be the work
of saints to be theologically relevant. [3] The way in
which the "official" Church has condemned, or, worse still,
ignored these phenomena is very harmful to the unity of the
Church. Better take a risk and deal with embarrassing problems of this kind than create the impression that there's
nothing the matter and let the institution and the inspiration drift further and further apart. In this sense, too,
"truthfulness" is "the future of the Church."

34

variably consist of Christians who, without giving
up their loyalty to their several churches, come
together on an interdenominational basis to have a
meal in which they prayerfully share bread and
wine as a re-enactment of Jesus' suffering and
death and resurrection, and with an express appeal
to his institution. Celebrations like these are
clearly gestures that involve a profession of
faith. Not only do they point to, and even to an
extent realize, the union of Christians, they are
also the expression of a very specific concern
with the world and its problems — they interpret
life in terms of the life and death of Jesus and
the commitment that follows from the resurrection.

It is interesting to watch how the prevalent
church order does not know what to do with this
simple fact. The church order is used to asking
questions like: "Is this a Catholic or a Protestant service?" — "Is the person who says the words
of institution validly ordained?" — "Do all those
people believe in the real presence?" — "Do they
believe that the Eucharist is a sacrifice?" It is
clear what all these questions assume, namely,
that the reality of a sacrament can be entirely
brought within the ambit of definition and legis-
lation. The members of our groups, however, even
when pressed for an answer, usually refuse to go
beyond saying: "We do what Jesus Christ ordered us
to do." Very importantly, they usually neither
deny nor affirm any specific tenets from the tra-
tional credal statements about the Eucharist. [33]
Neither do the members insist on taking a polemic
or propagandistic stand with regard to the prevailing official church orders as such, nor do
they usually take sides for or against particular
church doctrines — they are only moderately in-
terested in them. The way they celebrate their
"sacraments", however, does agree with the perspectives of an up-to-date, more personalistic and
communitarian sacramental theology: they are mean-

---

33. This issue raises the question of the possibility
of a "return" to the "ante-predicative situation," to be
discussed below, pp. 69ff., 73-74.

ingful gestures rather than instrumental causes;
they are based on a real Christian commitment and
add to its inspiration; they are celebrations rather than "means"; they are experienced as true
only in so far as the participants interpret them
in terms of a mission in the world, in Jesus'
name. [34]

The question is, of course: If these blurred
and hazy and fugitive practices are to be considered part of the Church's reality, is there any
point in maintaining the idea that there should —
or even can — be any church order? It would seem
that this question, again, is largely one of assumptions. In terms of the prevalent church order
it is, of course, rather difficult to conceive of
a different one. Still, it does seem possible to
give a few indications of a new-style church order.

The church order of the future will have to
indulge to a less extent that lawyers' yearning
for ever-increasing legal refinement. No legal
system can ever hope to provide for all of life's
eventualities; *a fortiori*, an ecclesiastical legal
system that wants to remain evangelical will have
to be particularly careful not to quench the Spirit
who blows where he wills. Concretely, this means
that the church order will have to be viewed as
relative. It may never be completely identified
with the reality of Church and Sacrament, not only
qualitatively, but also extensively: there will
be things *outside* the church order. In other
words, initiatives *praeter ius* [35], no matter how

---

34. Again, this is not an uncritical eulogy of the so-
called underground church, in which we can find, unfortunately, all too many churchy hangups of the institutional
church alive and kicking, only turned inside out, so to
speak — sacramental self-gratification being perhaps the
most prominent of all. Saying this, however, is not to imply that the underground church is unimportant. Rather, I
think, it should be viewed as one of the laboratories of the
Church of the future, though a somewhat primitive one because
the main body and the authorities do not show enough interest and do not provide it with enough theological funds.

35. This expression refers to those things which, though

ambiguous they may seem, must be respected as a matter of course, [36] and the notion of *consuetudo contra ius* — a custom that goes against the law but which deserves standing on account of the acceptance it enjoys — needs to be elaborated. This is the same as saying that personal and communal choice will have to be protected by the church order in the future, [37] which will also help remind those who abide by the church order and who advocate its blessings that salvation is not identical with orthodoxy and church order.

All of these considerations, it will be realized, are based on an *option*, and this option is one in favor of a "Confessional Church", and *in that sense* against a popular, conventional Church. [38] This chapter may not end without at least a brief outline of an explanation of this option.

---

not felt to be strictly in keeping with the church order, are nevertheless not strictly against it either, but are felt to "bypass" it. This may be due to the fact that the church order has no provisions dealing with the case in hand, or because the existing provisions are felt not to apply in a particular situation. Cf. below, pp. 88ff., 137ff..

36. The unsatisfactoriness of the present situation is perhaps nowhere more clearly demonstrated than on this point. The notion of "experiment", for instance, is only verbally recognized by the Roman and most diocesan curias. Experiments are at the very least by definition *praeter ius*; they may even be *contra ius*, or look that way; but that is not necessarily evil either, except to those observers whose imagination and capacity for surrender have ceased to exceed the bounds of law.

37. Cf. Harvey Cox, *The Secular City*, Macmillan Paperback, New York, 1965, pp. 41-49, esp. 47.

38. It hardly needs emphasizing that the words "in that sense" are essential in this sentence. An "option against the popular Church" in the sense of a high-handed and callous imposition, on the broad masses of the faithful, of the duty to make completely personal choices would be entirely contrary to what I mean. But the prospect of a Church *in diaspora* makes it unwarranted to go on repeating *ad nauseam* the clerical phrase that "the simple faithful" must not be "disturbed." The Grand Inquisitor may not find

Church and World

The Pastoral Constitution on the Church in the
Modern World, *Gaudium et Spes*, of the second Vatican Council, has, as a matter of principle, abandoned the conception of the Church and civil soci-
ty as two "perfect societies" — *societates per-
fectae*. The categories in which it describes the
relationship between Church and world have become
more dynamic and also more evangelical. They are
based on the idea that God has chosen to reconcile
the world to himself in Christ, the Son of his favor, and that therefore the Christian faith of the
Church and of each Christian is a way, an *exodus*,
a process of growth through testing, a dynamism.
Expressions like "the servant Church," "the Church
as the sacrament of the Kingdom," and "God's People
on the way" place the Church and the Christian fundamentally outside the dilemma of the double allegiance. The Church is the voice of one crying in
the world: while being continually called together
and assembled on the basis of the free obedience of
faith, the Church may never present its own order
as a counterpart of the civil order. Church order
should be fundamentally preaching and not forcing,
challenging and not patronizing, making free and
not numbing. But the order we are still living
with today is in many ways still the legal system
of the perfect society, which has no way of dealing with, let alone welcoming, the broadening two-
way traffic-area between the Church(es) and the
world, which is the vital development of the last,
let us say, twenty or thirty years. What we see
is no longer the fringe tugging at the center of

---

a hearing, today less than ever; a patient but resolute effort must be made to make nothing less than the truth available to the faithful at large. I have tried to state my
views on this transition from popular Church to confessional
Church under cover of an article on "The Practice of Obedience and Authority in the Dutch Catholic Church," in: J.
Dalrymple *et al.*, *Authority in a Changing Church*, London,
1968, pp. 138-161.

the Church, but the outside air being felt throughout the Church. In a very real way, the tables
have been turned: canon law and order is no longer
judging the world, but they themselves are being
subjected to criticism arising from the fact that
the civil order wants to be taken seriously before
it lets itself be taught.

It would seem to be in order, incidentally,
for the Church to remind herself at this point
that it would be a caricature of reality if she
were to think that civil legal order is entirely
based on the power of the letter and tradition and
convention, and that church order should be of a
totally different nature, having nothing in common
with the civil legal order. In the spirit of *Gaudium et Spes* the ideal would be for the church order to
be the paradigm of a truly redeemed legal order.

Unfortunately, the reverse is often the case.
Documents such as the Declaration on Human Rights,
activities like those attempting to gain more effective freedom of expression and demonstration,
and criticizing the idea that institutional authority must always be presumed to act legitimately,
protests against secrecy and censorship, against
rigoristic divorce laws, against an absolute ban
on homosexual practices and on contraceptives —
these and so many other events show that there are
forces at work in society which tend to give more
leeway to the freedom of the citizen. There is a
pervasive trust, apparently, that the democratiza-
tion of the social institutions has set free the
personal responsibility of the citizen to a larger
extent than the law has been prepared to allow so
far. If civil law makes it possible for the citizen of the Secular City to make more conscientious
decisions of his own without fear of jeopardizing
the common good, how much more urgent a need there
is for the church order to respect "the freedom of
the Christian person"! It is frightening at times
to watch the civil legal order trying to take the
citizen's heightened sense of social responsibility
and identity more and more seriously, whereas the
church order seems to go on and on protecting, pa-

tronizing, clarifying, refining, defining and pre-
scribing. Should not the church order be the pro-
totype of the most fully redeemed legal order rather than the civil order?

This is, then, also the reason why this chapter started with a reference to the demands made
on the church order by society today and even more
so by society tomorrow. If the renewal of the
Church does not base itself firmly and unequivocally on the social awareness and the sense of i-
dentity of the free citizen in the making, then
she will become more and more the haven of the so-
cially retarded, spellbound by the power of the
establishment and the vested interests advocating
law and order — content to live under an anaes-
thesia that is disguised as safety and security.
A Church that fails to challenge will develop into an accomplice of the world. Its God will be
little more than the warrant for a stable, un-
changing social order, and its members will be the
slaves of the great powers and conventions: sta-
tus-seeking, yearning for respectability, adverti-
zing, law and order: the patronizers of the enslaved consumer. This may sound dangerously (and
maybe even a bit fashionably) countercultural, but
it does at least convey that faith is not a consu-
mer-good. The Church in the City of the future
will have to appeal to the awakening desire of
countless people to seek deliverance from these
powers, which Paul would certainly have called the
"elements of this world." [39] And the Church
will only be able to do this if the church order
does not even give the semblance of being an ecclesiastical version of an established civil order. Nothing but the free acceptance of our res-
cue, by Christ, from the powers that be — a res-
cue kept alive in the Church and her holy celebrations — will be able to make Church membership
meaningful to the enslaved but inwardly rebelling
consumer.

---

39. Cf. Gal 4, 3. 9.

TWO:

Validity and Invalidity

EVER SINCE Augustine, at the end of the fourth century, developed his doctrine about Christ's presence in the sacraments and thus made the most significant contribution to the settlement of the dispute about Baptism administered by heretics, it seemed that the Church had a criterion at once simple and profound by which to judge the value of Baptism administered outside the Unity of the Church — the *Unitas Ecclesiae* so cherished by Cyprian. There arose a few different formulations of the principle uncovered by Augustine; one of them was "the intention of doing what the Church does" (*intentio faciendi quod facit Ecclesia*), another was "the minister's faithful adherence to the essential rite" (as, for instance, though in a different context, DS 3874). Still, whatever the formulation, the Church seemed settled in her recognition of Christ's activity in Baptism, even in cases where the doctrinal ideas behind baptismal practices were dubious or even heretical (*e.g.*, Subordinationism, Macedonianism, heretical doctrine about justification). [1]

This recognition, of course, had a much wider

---

1. In pondering such a sweeping survey of church history as contained in this paragraph and the next, I have come to agree with my friend John Coventry, S. J., when he writes: "One becomes more and more convinced that there is a need of a serious and full-length study of the meaning of the word "validity" throughout the Church's history and in various areas of thought. Such a study would prove to be not merely a scholarly exercise, but of considerable value to ecumenical discussions." See "Valid," *Faith and Unity* 12(1968)91-93, quotation 91.

Grounded in Love

scope than Baptism; it applied in principle to all
sacraments administered outside the unity of the
Church. This accounts for the fact that there has
never been any serious doubt concerning the sacraments of the Eastern Orthodox Churches, nor have
important doctrinal differences (such as that a-
bout the consecratory efficacy of the *epiclesis* in
the Eucharist: cf. DS 3556 and note) ever been in
the way of the Catholic Church's recognition of
the validity of these sacraments.

This radical stand on the part of the Church,
however, is as dangerous as it is comforting, for
the only alternative to an unqualified Yes is a
peremptory No. The latter stand was actually taken at the time of the Reformation, and thus a
wholly novel situation arose with regard to the
validity of sacraments. For Protestant Baptism
the Church could, thank God, fall back upon her
radical recognition of Baptism administered outside the unity of the Church. [2] Neither did
Marriage present a difficulty; all Trent did was
prescribe a particular canonical form to be observed by all Catholics, and make the validity of
the Marriage dependent on that form. The fact
that, roughly speaking, the Reformation did not
recognize Matrimony as a sacrament instituted by
Christ did not detract from its validity in the
eyes of the Catholic Church, since every marriage-
bond between baptized partners was by that very
fact a sacrament.

The rest of the sacraments fell into two
classes. The Eucharist was generally accepted by
the Reformation as a sacrament instituted by
Christ; the other sacraments were — although in
varying degrees — discarded. But now a case presented itself for which the traditional approach
had made only very indirect provisions. The vali-

─────────────────

2. One could, incidentally, go on to ask whether the
circumstance that the issue of the valid sacrament outside
the Church was almost entirely fought on the field of Baptism did not in fact contribute to a narrowing of the Church's
awareness whenever the validity of other sacraments outside
the unity of the Church became an issue.

42

dity of the Eucharist (and of Confirmation and the
sacraments of Penance, Order, and the Anointing of
the Sick) had always been made dependent on the
intention of the minister (the issue of the intention of the recipient need not be considered in
this context); but now that the sacrament of Order
was dropped in the vast majority of Protestant
Churches the sacramental *competence* of the minister disappeared, and this became the new reason
for the Catholic Church to pronounce her verdict
of *invalidum*.

How did the Roman Catholic Church come to es-
tablish the sacramental incompetence of the Protestant ministry? First of all, from the mouths
of most of the Reformers themselves, who did not
recognize ordination to the ministry as necessary
or sacramental. Yet, to provide for the border-
case of the Anglican Church, and to gain some more
insight into the reasoning behind the verdict of
invalidity, let us ask ourselves the following
question. If the Reformation had accepted the
sacrament of Order, would in that case the ministry of the Eucharist — even if the Reformation,
broadly speaking, had maintained its stand against
Confirmation, Penance, and Anointing of the Sick —
have been valid? The Roman Catholic Church's answer to this question was given in the Letter *Apostolicae Curae*, promulgated by Pope Leo XIII on
September 13, 1896, in which validity is denied to
Anglican Orders on account of a defect of form
(*defectus formae*) as well as a defect of intention
(*defectus intentionis*) in the ordination. With
regard to the latter we must observe the following.
The original drafters of the *Form and Manner of
Making, Ordaining and Consecrating of Bishops,
Priests and Deacons* (three versions: 1549, 1552,
1662; the 1552 one is the most anti-Roman) did not
recognize the sacrament of Order; Thomas Cranmer
in particular, as Dom Gregory Dix has observed,
"was probably seriously heretical about the meaning of Ordination." This is confirmed by *Articles
of Religion* XXVIII and XXXI, which contain strongly anti-Roman statements about the Eucharist, so

43

that the inference is inescapable that the ritual
intended to exclude such an ordination as would
authorize the ordinand to offer the eucharistic
sacrifice. Finally, the *forma* — that is to say,
the words that convey the essential meaning of the
sacramental ritual — is purposely deficient in
respect to the eucharistic sacrifice.

Hence, when the question is asked just where
the heresy about the sacrament of Order and the
deficiency of the ordination ritual is located,
the Roman Catholic Church has answered that the
Anglican doctrine about the *Eucharist* is defective: all references to the sacrificial nature of
the Eucharist have been removed from the sacrament
of Order and its ritual. Now it so happens that
the sacrament of Order is "principally" (*praecipu-
e*) defined by the "power to consecrate and offer
the Lord's true Body and Blood" (*potestas consecrandi et offerendi verum corpus et sanguinem Domini* — DS 3316). Consecration and sacrifice,
however, are repudiated by the makers of the Ordinal and by *Articles* XXVIII and XXXI, and purposely passed over in the ordination ritual. The
essence of the sacrament of Order, therefore, dis-
appears, so that the ordinations are invalid, and
with the ordinations all other sacraments administered by Anglican ministers, especially the Eucharist. [3]

---

3. The best authority on the question of Anglican orders at the present moment is still Dr. John Jay Hughes, at
one time an Anglican priest, who was conditionally ordained
to the priesthood in the Roman Catholic Church by the bishop of Münster in 1968. His book, *Absolutely Null and Utterly Void, The Papal Condemnation of Anglican Orders, 1896*
(Washington - Cleveland, 1968), is a highly professional as
well as entertaining treatment of the history behind the
papal condemnation. On pp. 284-293 Hughes brings up some
of the issues involved in any reappraisal of Anglican orders, and especially discusses the two books by Francis
Clark, *Anglican Orders and Defect of Intention* and *Eucharistic Sacrifice and the Reformation*. On this subject, cf.
also Hughes' own articles listed in his prodigious biblio-
graphy, on p. 324. Dr. Hughes has given us a second volume,

It is important to realize how far we have
traveled from the case of Baptism administered by
heretics. The sacramental ministry of the most
"churchy" Church of the Reformation is invalidated
on the grounds of the incompetence of its ministers, which in turn is ultimately based on a heretical doctrine of that particular sacrament which
is at the heart of the ministry as it is at the
heart of the Church. The answer to our question,
therefore, is: even in the Anglican Church, which
in some real sense knows and acknowledges the sacrament of Order (witness, for instance, the Pre-
face to the Ordinal), the post-baptismal sacraments are invalid. [4]
    With this, we have laid down one element of
our point of departure for the remainder of this
book. The Roman Catholic Church has unambiguously
pronounced the hard sentence of *invalidum* on the
post-baptismal sacramental ministry of the Reformation.

---

dealing with the validity of the arguments against Anglican
orders, and entitled *Stewards of the Lord* (London, 1970).
    4. On an overall view of the ecumenical situation there
seems to be no reason to be unduly embarrassed with this verdict of *invalidum*. It could well be a major temptation to
tackle the ecumenical dialogue and set out on the road to u-
nity almost entirely from the viewpoint of Faith and Order.
In other words, if — whether successfully or not — we were
to try to talk Anglican orders into validity in the Roman
Catholic sense, we might very well find ourselves tempted to
close the door behind (or in front of) the Anglicans with the
final verdict: Romans, Orthodox, Old Catholics (and Anglicans) have valid orders, and the rest don't; the latter,
therefore, have no post-baptismal sacraments. For the present writer the experience of the beauty and truth of Anglican
worship, added to his awareness that this sacramental ministry is at present widely considered invalid in Roman Catholic terms, has been the principal stimulus to elaborate a
somewhat broader view of the sacraments outside the Church —
one which would include, not exclude, the post-baptismal sacraments of the non-episcopal churches of the Reformation.

Grounded in Love

Validity and invalidity:
their role in the celebration of a sacrament

The post-baptismal sacraments in the churches of
the Reformation are invalid. Still, there are not
nothing. What, then, *are* they? This question is
the second element of our point of departure. It
will encourage us to seek positive answers rather
than dwell on a negative verdict.

There is no quick way to a satisfactory answer in this area. Only careful, patient analysis
will lead to insight, and chapters III and IV will
be devoted to that. To bring this chapter to a
close, let us try to decide what the verdict of
invalidity really entails — in other words, what
"valid" and "invalid" practically mean in the celebration of sacraments. After that, we will briefly review some Catholic evaluations of Protestant
sacraments.

The first feature we must notice is that under normal circumstances the validity of a sacrament plays no part whatever in the consciousness
of the congregation and the minister celebrating
it. No matter how profound and fundamental a reality the validity of a sacrament may be, there is
always something incongruous and even contradict-
ory about it; this is so because it puts in relief
the fact that God's sovereign mercy can *overcome*
barriers raised by those who celebrate the sacrament. The notion of validity comes to the fore
only in paradoxical situations. That the Donatist
Baptism could not be repeated was such a harrowing
doctrine for Augustine to teach because of the
painful contradiction involved in it: those baptized in the Donatist church were incorporated into Christ while consciously withdrawing from his
body, the Church. In the same way, the unworthy
minister or recipient of the Eucharist is guilty
of profaning the body he belongs to and the blood
poured out for his salvation; he eats and drinks
judgment upon himself — the sacrament turns a-
gainst him. Similarly, the validity of a marriage
becomes an issue the moment the partners begin to

46

consider a divorce. [5]

A parallel reasoning can be set up for the invalid sacrament. No one is prepared so unconditionally and absolutely to rely on sacramental validity or *opus operatum* for his salvation as to make it impossible for sacramental salvation to exist outside the strictly valid sacrament. One day a student asked Karl Rahner in class whether a priest would be validly ordained even if in the chain of episcopal consecrations leading up to his ordaining bishop there had once been an objectively invalid consecration. Rahner reportedly replied that one should not think about these things *so apothekerhaft* — as if we were dealing with a chemical-pharmaceutical proposition. Here again we can say that the invalidity of a sacrament becomes relevant only in paradoxical situations: the priest who turns out to have been invalidly ordained after a lifetime of fruitful ministry; the happy parents who discover, on the eve. of their golden jubilee, that they were invalidly married; and so on. But these are exceptions; in normal situations nobody worries about the possible validity or invalidity of sacraments he or she either received or administered.

Finally, we have the fact that "doubtfully valid" sacraments are possible — the assumption being, of course, that they would be fruitful in any case. Thus, for instance, the introductory prescriptions about the Mass in the old Roman Missal (known in some quarters as "the Missal of St. Pius V" nowadays), *De defectibus in celebratione missae*, mention a number of cases in which the celebration of the Eucharist would be of doubtful validity. [6] Furthermore, any textbook of Roman

---

5. It is clear that the paradox of a merely valid sacrament must not be driven too far. God's sovereign power is never diametrically opposed to human intention and the situations created by the latter. In doctrinal terms, intention is requisite for any sacrament; without intention of doing what the Church does (*intentio faciendi quod facit ecclesia*) there can be no sacrament at all.

6. Cf., *e.g.*, III, 3; the doubt is about the quality

Catholic moral theology will furnish the reader
with any number of *dubia* — debatable cases — regarding the validity of sacraments. One famous
case is the one in which two people, one of whom
is doubtfully impotent — a real impotence is a
ground for nullity! — are authorized by the bishop to get married. It seems clear that one can
lead a sacramental life without the assurance that
the validity of each individual sacrament can be
established with mechanical (or magical?) preci-
sion.

It is understandable that Roman Catholic
practice has always insisted that doubtfully valid
and invalid sacraments, if and when discovered, be
convalidated. This convalidation does not imply
that "there has been nothing so far," but it does
make sense for fruitful sacramental celebrations
of salvation to receive the formal endorsement of
the Church. What remains important is this: the
Church appears to have a healthy awareness of the
relative value of the notions of validity and invalidity in sacramental matters. Validity is no
more (and no less) than juridical ecclesiastical
recognition of a true sacrament. It is the fin-
ishing touch every normal sacramental celebration
needs as its marginal rounding-off. One logical
conclusion to be drawn from this is the following. Validity involves the Church's assurance
that a celebration is indeed a true sacrament.
Invalidity merely withholds that assurance; it
does not positively involve the Church's assurance that a celebration is not a true sacrament in
the sense of not being a cause and sign of Christ's
gracious presence.[7]

---

of the altarbreads.

7. These final sentences represent a correction of the
text as it appeared in previous publications. The article
by John Coventry quoted on p. 41, note 1 is mainly responsible for this change. I originally wrote: "Validity is no
more (and no less) than the juridical claim to ecclesiastical recognition." This is ambiguous. I agree with Coventry
when he writes: "The purpose of this article is to suggest
that, at least in view of the many different senses that the

Traditional Roman theology, however, with its strong Scotistic and legal background, has always suffered from a certain amount of *naiveté* characteristic of lawyers. It has always had a tendency to identify the whole sacrament with its minimal status, the valid sacrament. There is a bit of faulty logic at the basis of this equation, and it more or less runs as follows. The minimal (= merely valid) sacrament is a true sacrament, so the essential is contained in the minimal. Conclusion: the essential sacrament *is* the minimal sacrament, and everything that goes beyond mere validity is no longer essential, no longer sacrament, but mere devotion, recipient's disposition, fruit, *supererogatio*. [8]

---

word has had in the course of the Church's history, it has now come to be used, and can only be used without confusion, in one specific sense: to say that a sacrament is valid is to say precisely that one's church recognizes it; [...] Validity is not some obscure metaphysical and unobservable entity, which the Church is trying to discover in a sacrament, in order to make up her mind whether to call it valid or not. [...] when the Church is trying to make up her mind whether a sacrament is valid, she is intent on discovering whether it has all the other qualities that she would expect in order to give it her recognition." (*O.c.*, pp. 91-92.) Cf. also above, p. 25ff.

    8. The same tendency can be observed at the level of ritual. The precise definition of the matter and form of the sacrament of Order (DS 3857-3861) and the devotion to the "naked moment of consecration" are the fruits of similar processes of feeling and reasoning. In the ordination-rite the laying-on of hands by the bishop is minimal and therefore also essential; but does that mean that for that reason the participating priests are no more than an ornament, as *e.g.* John Bligh, following a host of other writers, suggests in *Ordination to the Priesthood* (London, 1956, pp. 92-96)? Here as everywhere the precisely defined minimal rite becomes relevant only in paradoxical situations. Cf., in this context, also the tendency to present infant Baptism as the sacrament *par excellence*: maximal emphasis on the *opus operatum*, minimal *opus operantis*. But in all these cases we should remind ourselves that from an overstatement of the

Grounded in Love

In the last few decades a better, more existential type of sacramental theology has arisen. It
has been re-discovered that the merely valid sacrament is a limit — in fact, that it is the lowest
possible limit. In normal circumstances the sacraments are not just taken to be claims to official
juridical recognition, entitling the recipient to
being considered a church member in good standing.
Sacraments are also, and in the first place, rites
in which Christians share in the Church's and
Christ's own worship offered to the Father, and in
which they participate, with Christ, in the gracious communion with the Father and the Spirit.
[9]. This means that a sacrament becomes more of
a sacrament, not less, according as the mere limit
of validity is exceeded. [10] Just as the order
of justice is based on the order of charity, and
not the other way round, the validity of a sacrament is normally a consequence of personal appro-
priation, celebration, and reception of a sacrament, not its basis. The truly fruitful sacrament
— in Thomas Aquinas' terms, the level of *sacramentum et res* — is the vital core of the sacrament; mere validity is only its paradoxical limit.
[11]

The merely valid sacrament, we have stated,
occurs only in paradoxical situations, which most-

---

validity and *opus operatum* aspects it takes but one step to
the thesis that sacraments are basically not "received" but
"incurred," so to speak. Cf. above, pp. 14–23.

9. Cf. above, p. 12, note 2.

10. Cf. the way in which the Decree on Justification of
the Council of Trent emphasizes the freedom and the personal
cooperation of the person who receives salvation. Cf. above,
p. 26, note 20.

11. That validity is the limit of fruitfulness is very
clear from the fact that the merely valid, non-fruitful sacrament is ambivalent. On the one hand such a sacrament turns
against the recipient ("eats and drinks judgement upon himself"); it becomes a counter-sign of salvation. On the other
hand it remains an invitation to repentance and conversion;
the latter is the specific "fruit" of the "merely valid" sacrament. Purely neutral sacraments do not exist.

50

ly, though not always, involves bad faith on the part of those administering and/or receiving the sacrament. This is not the place to decide whether such bad faith has ever been, or can ever be, a matter of actual fact. This much is certain, however: Augustine pictures the Donatists as Christians in bad faith, and the Council of Trent, even in its less polemic sessions, does pretty much the same with regard to the Reformers. Still, when Augustine holds Donatist baptisms to be valid, he does so because he is aware that these baptisms can lay a strict claim to recognition by the Church, even though those who celebrate them are in bad faith. But what are we to say about sacraments received and administered by people in good faith — members of a *bona fide* Church? To put this in recognized terminology, what to make of sacraments celebrated, not by people who intentionally teach different doctrine (*haeretici formales*), but by people who teach doctrine which only in fact is different (*haeretici materiales*)? Could we perhaps say that in such cases we are back to the normal situation, in which salvation is celebrated and signified without so much as a thought about validity or invalidity in the minds of those taking part?

This first, very tentative question requires a first, very tentative exploration into the status of the sacraments in the churches of the Reformation.

Current evaluations of Protestant sacraments

In two directions, roughly speaking, the more cautious among Roman Catholic theologians have sought to answer the question about the value of post-baptismal Protestant sacraments. [12] These sacraments, it has been said, do not celebrate salva-

---

12. The matter comes, of course, to a head in the Eucharist, the only sacrament administered by all Protestant churches. However, by using the plural "sacraments", we expressly wish to include all High-Church tendencies, especially in the Anglican Communion.

tion really, but spiritually ("Christ is not really, but spiritually present in the Lord's Supper in the Protestant Church"). Alternatively, Protestant sacraments have been described as sacraments by virtue of aspiration (*sacramentum in voto* or *votum sacramenti*).

The former of these suggestions is, of course, most unfortunately worded, to say the least. In Scripture everything in which the Spirit plays a part is pre-eminently real: "The Egyptians are men, and not God; and their horses are flesh, and not Spirit" (Isaiah 31, 3). "It is the Spirit that gives life, the flesh is of no avail; the words that I have spoken to you are Spirit and life" (John 6, 63). The separation between "spiritual" and "real", which the formula suggests as the key to a solution, is based on untenable assumptions. One assumption is that "spiritual" is tantamount to "unreal" or "metaphorical". It might be worth investigating how much this assumption owes to the scholastic debate about the *universalia*; in any case it must be said that the classical term *physice*, which can mean "really" as well as "materially", has played an important and highly confusing part in traditional theology, and contributed not a little to relegating the spiritual to the realm of (more or less pious) imagination and metaphor. Added to this, there was the confusion between the biblical idea of "spiritual" (which Calvin stressed so consistently) and the scholastic, technical meaning of the term. Finally, there was the tacit, widespread assumption that grace is a "purely spiritual" entity, "caused" by a sacramental rite. As a result, the formula "spiritual, not real" tended to drive the sacrament entirely in the direction of the material rite, where the reality of the sacrament was conceived of as massively concentrated (and which was viewed almost exclusively as an instrumental cause, at the expense of its value as a sign). From there, it took only one more step to consider the *opus operatum*, the *sacramentum tantum*, as the "real" thing, and to oppose it, as such, to the "spiri-

tual" import of the rite, the *res sacramenti*. Once
this stage has been reached, "real" will tend to
get identified with "material", leaving nothing but
unreality to the "spiritual". Once the dilemma
had been put this way, the Reformers (except Lu-
ther and his immediate followers) opted for "spiritual, not real", especially in matters pertain-
ing to the Eucharist [*13*], and the Roman Catholics
for "sacramental — but with a tendency to a one-
sided emphasis on the material *opus operatum* —
and real".

In light of a somewhat more human sacramental
theology, which has re-discovered the spiritual
sign-value of the material rite and the incarna-
tional nature of grace, we must reject the alternative "*physice* and real" as against "spiritual
and not real". The whole point of a sacrament,

---

13. For the sake of exposition I have, of course, sim-
plified matters considerably. In the Reformers' discussions
about the Eucharistic presence we actually find *two* strands
of thought continually intertwined. On the one hand there
is the completely justifiable appeal to the realistic meaning of the word "spiritual" in Scripture. Calvin hints at
this in *Institutio* IV, xvii, 10. 32-33; and Bishop Guest,
the author of the revised version of Article XXVIII in 1563,
commented upon the words, "The Body of Christ is given, taken, and eaten, in the Supper, only after an heavenly and
spiritual manner," by saying that the formula did not mean
"to exclude the Presence of Christ's Body from the Sacrament,
but only the grossness and sensibleness in the receiving
thereof." The second strain of thought was propagated especially by the Zürich Reformers against Roman and Lutheran realism with regard to the Lord's Supper, by reviving Berengar
and denying "anye reall and essencial presence there beeyng
of Christ's naturall fleshe and bloude" (Black Rubric, *Book
of Common Prayer*, edition of 1552). The argument ran as follows: "... the truth of man's nature requireth, that the
body of one and the selfsame man cannot be at one time in di-
verse places, but must needs be in some one certain place:
[...] And because [...] Christ was taken up into heaven [...]
a faithful man ought not either to believe or openly to con-
fess the real and bodily presence [...] of Christ's flesh and
blood, in the sacrament of the Lord's Supper" (Art. XLII, 1552).

as of every human, interpersonal gesture, is precisely the affectively experienced unity of the
spiritual and the material [*14*]. Augustine for-
mulates this as follows: a sign is "something
which, apart from the impression it makes on the
senses, causes, of itself, something else to come
to awareness as well." [*15*] In traditional terms:
the theology of the sacraments must base itself on
a consideration of the meaningful rite *as a whole*,
on the *sacramentum et res*, which is the heart of
the sacramental celebration, with at one extreme
the mere limit of the valid *opus operatum*, and on
the other extreme the mere limit of the so-called
purely spiritual grace, the *res sacramenti*. If,
therefore, one were to insist that Protestant sacraments celebrate salvation spiritually, one cannot help saying at the same time that they are
real sacraments. In the concrete order, a purely
spiritual economy of grace is impossible. Sacraments are human gestures, and they follow the laws
of human gestures in that sign and meaning are
given as one. They are, of course, more than merely human gestures, for they come to be in the power
of the Spirit; in the latter sense they are indeed
"purely spiritual".

A more understanding note is sounded by the
second evaluation proposed by some Roman Catholic
theologians with regard to the post-baptismal sacraments in the Protestant churches, namely, that
they are sacraments by aspiration, *in voto*. [*16*]

14. It is precisely the absence of any human dimension
that makes the three canons of the Inquisition, issued under
Pope Gregory XI to deal with the problem of the Eucharistic
presence (DS 1101-1103), so gross and so offensive.

15. *Res praeter speciem quam ingerit sensibus aliud
aliquid ex se faciens in cogitationem venire.* — Quoted in
P. Smulders, "Symbolisch tekengebruik," *Bijdragen* 17(1956)
152-161; quotation 153. Note the word "awareness" (*cogitationem*), which in Augustine's idiom denotes a much more fully human activity than the Thomistic term "knowledge" (*cog-
nitionem*) usually found in the textbooks.

16. Harry J. McSorley, writing in *The Ecumenist* 5(1967)
68-75, points out that "the idea of a *votum sacramenti* was a

Still, the formula is a dangerous one. Is not its
obvious exegesis: a desire for the sacrament — so
no sacrament? But if the formula were understood
in this fashion, we would again be separating the
activity of the recipient (his *votum*) from what
would presumably have to be the "sacrament proper"
— which would again, by implication, be reduced
to a mere *opus operatum*. But the expression "sacrament by aspiration" affords another possibility,
although this may at first blush seem to stretch
the formula a bit. Could the formula not be taken
to mean: "a desire of the valid sacrament," and
even: "a desire for the recognition of the sacrament"? If the dispositions of the minister and the
recipients are under normal circumstances co-con-
stitutive for the sacrament; if the aspirations of
a *bona fide* community celebrating a sacrament make
the rite more, not less, of a sacrament: could it

---

familiar, pre-conciliar notion" (74). By a careful analysis
of the text of the Decree on Ecumenism, § 22, of the *modi*
offered in the conciliar discussions, and of the responses
given by the Secretariate for Christian Unity, he arrives at
the conclusion that "the intention of the Decree is to affirm that Protestant Churches have in their celebration of
the Lord's Supper *something* of the reality of the eucharistic mystery" (*Ibid.*). The expression is, of course, not very
precise, but it helps to convey that it is dubious theology
to define the sacraments in such a way that they must necessarily be placed *in indivisibili*; cf. above, p. 21. — On
this point, therefore, I have to disagree with George H. Tavard, when he writes: "Some would like to point out that
[the Decree's reference to] the lack of 'the genuine and integral substance' does not rule out the presence of *some*
substance of the eucharistic mystery and that, accordingly,
the Council recognizes the substance of the eucharist (though
not 'genuine and integral') in Protestant communities. But
this does not help. For the eucharistic reality that is recognized here by the Council is no more than the 'profession
that life in Christ is then symbolized and his glorious coming is expected.' It refers to a subjective persuasion of
piety, not to an objective liturgical fact." ("Does the Protestant Ministry Have Sacramental Significance?", *Continuum*
6(1968)260-269; quotation 264.)

not be said, then, that the vital core of the sacrament, the *sacramentum et res*, is realized? Could
it be said that such a sacrament is only waiting
for the Catholic Church to recognize it?

These are the questions which we should like
to ask at greater length in the next two chapters.

THREE:

Church and Church Doctrine

OVER THE last few decades Roman Catholic thinking
on ecumenical matters has taken a turn that amounts
to a conversion. The evidence for this conversion
is obviously not in the first place found in official documents, but in the living *sensus catholi-
cus* of an increasing number of Roman Catholics.
Yet, since the promulgation, at the second Vatican
Council, of the Decree on Ecumenism *Unitatis Redintegratio*, it has become possible to trace this
exciting development even at the highest, official
level. If Pope John XXIII used preferably to refer to "separated brethren" — *fratres separati* —
Paul VI, in his opening address to the second session, used the term "Christian communions" — *com-
muniones christianae* — and at the start of the
third session even "churches" — *ecclesiae* —,
which latter two expressions found their way into
the Decree on Ecumenism. [1] This may appear to
be a matter of simple politeness and charity, but
on closer scrutiny the implications of this usage
might well in the end amount to a landslide.
    Up to less than twenty years ago the ecumen-
ical interest among Roman Catholics stood under
the heavy pressure of an ominous question: How
is it possible to conceive of reunion in terms
other than those of a *return* to the *existing* unity of the *Catholica*? There always was scope, at
least in principle, for far-reaching concessions
in the areas of liturgy, relatively independent
government, and local piety, but the central de-

---

1. Cf., *e.g.*, § 3. By contrast, the Code of Canon Law
refers to "non-Catholic sects" (*sectae acatholicae*) and to
"heretical or schismatic sects" (*sectae haereticae seu
schismaticae*): canons 1065 § 1; 1060.

mand was uncompromising: in virtue of what seemed
to be an inevitable theological necessity, those
who had separated themselves from the Catholic
Church had to return to her. It looked wellnigh
impossible to conceive of reunion otherwise than
as a restoration of the state of affairs before
the disruption, except that, of course, the
"churches" would have to endorse all the dogmatic
acquisitions that had occurred since the separation, especially the decrees of Trent and Vatican
I, and the two most recent Marian dogmas. This
theological vision was behind the overt attitude
of suspicion with regard to the ecumenical movement and especially the World Council of Churches.
To strive for unity outside the unity of the *Catholica* — again, conceived of as already extant
— could very easily be construed as an effort to
strive *against* the unity of the *Catholica*. [2]
This way of conceiving of the unity of Christ's
Church as absolute was based on a reasoning that
was generally accepted, especially in apologetics,
up to a few decades ago, and it ran as follows.
Christ willed and founded one Church. If one were
to set out on a search for the church that would
be able to substantiate every claim to that title,
one would necessarily come to identify the Church
founded by Christ as the Roman Catholic Church.
This church alone has always been consistent with
itself and in possession of the integral truth [3];

---

2. Cf. DS 2885-2888; 3300-3310, esp. 3304: "Christ's
Church, therefore, is one and enduring; all those who turn
elsewhere stray away from the will and command of Christ
the Lord, leave the road to salvation, and are on their way
to perdition." (*Est igitur Ecclesia Christi unica et perpe-
tua: quicumque seorsum eant, aberrant a voluntate et prae-
scriptione Christi Domini relictoque salutis itinere ad in-
teritum digrediuntur.*)
    3. Connected with this is the massive interpretation
of Vincent of Lerins' famous canon, laying down the rule
that what must be believed is "what [has been believed] at
all times, in all places, by all" (*quod semper quod ubique
quod ab omnibus*). This theory remained the single biggest
obstacle, long after the publication of Newman's *Essay on*

reunion, therefore, can basically be understood to
mean nothing but the restoration of the state of
affairs before the separation. In other words,
the theological view of reunion was characterized
by a retrospective, historical view of the wrongs
involved in the severance of all ties with the *Catholica*. The Faith and Order component in the ecumenical movement was watched with strong interest
and high hopes: once certain Protestant groups
would have rediscovered the full Creed and the hierarchical church order, they were bound to return
to the fold, as so many Tractarians had done in
the nineteenth century. [4] The Life and Work movement was viewed rather more sceptically; the
dangers of modernism, pragmatism and indifferent-
ism were only too obvious, as was the movement's
anti-Catholic bias. [5]
    Pope Pius XII's encyclical on the Mystical
Body, *Mystici Corporis*, of 1943, proposed a massive identification of the Roman Catholic Church
and the Mystical Body of Christ. In this way, the
encyclical also functioned as the justification,
on the Catholic Church's own terms, of her attitude toward the ecumenical movement. [6] The ful-

---

the Development of Christian Doctrine, to a realistic, organic theory about the evolution of the deposit of faith,
ever new and ever renewing itself. Cf. Owen Chadwick's fine
monograph on the subject: *From Bossuet to Newman, The Idea
of Doctrinal Development*, Cambridge, 1957.
    4. John Jay Hughes (*Absolutely Null and Utterly Void,
passim*) relates, not without some irony, how those in favor
of a condemnation of Anglican orders, especially Cardinal
Vaughan, used the prospect of numerous conversions as one of
their main arguments. However, they failed to appreciate
High Anglican sensibilities in this regard, and were proved
badly mistaken by history.
    5. For arguments in favor of a strong emphasis on Life
and Work, not only in terms of joint Christian action, but
also as an opportunity to attune the Christian response to
the secular environment, which acts as a challenge to existing church structures, cf. above, pp. 9-12, 32-40, and below,
pp. 137-148.
    6. Note that F. Malmberg, in his profound commentary

ly developed, hierarchically structured Church proposed to us in this important document does indeed represent a pinnacle of ecclesial awareness. Still, this should not blind us to the fact that in the concrete order *Mystici Corporis* painted far too eschatological a picture of the Church, and failed to distinguish between the Church and the Kingdom. This in turn brought about far too narrow a theological vision of the Church, resulting in too exclusive an attitude on the part of Catholic theology towards the ecumenical movement. [7]

Ecumenism:
a new orientation and a new conception of the Church

In the ecclesiological discussions of the last few decades, however, a lot of ground has been gained in favor of ideas which provide a definite complement to, if not a downright correction of, *Mystici Corporis*. [8] Thus we have, among other things,

---

on the encyclical, introduces a restriction on a few crucial points, *e.g.* in a passage like the following: "This means that the membership of [the Church's] members is imperfect, so that I will always and everywhere have to distinguish between 'the person *who* is a member' and 'the person *insofar as* he is a member* — between 'material' and 'formal' membership; and this imperfection of membership precisely expresses the difference between 'the Church *in via* [on the way]' and 'the Church *in patria* [in her heavenly home]'': *Ein Leib, ein Geist — Vom Mysterium der Kirche,* Freiburg - Basel - Wien, 1960, pp. 298-299 (my translation). On the same page 299, however, stronger emphasis is placed on the absolute holiness of the Church; could one here, too, introduce the clause, "*insofar as* she is really Church, eschatological People of God"?

7. Cf. Pope Pius XII.'s peremptory refusal to cooperate in any form with the World Council of Churches, expressed, among other instances, on the occasion of Bishop Otto Dibelius' ecumenical visit to the Vatican, in early 1956.

8. Cf. the opening address of Pope Paul VI on October 29, 1963: *Mystici Corporis* must be complemented. In saying this the Pope was endorsing conciliar discussions and anticipating the Dogmatic Constitution on the Church, *Lumen Gen-*

the "concentric" view of the Church and the idea
of the "People of God" as complements to the idea
of the Mystical Body. [9] It has been recognized
that the massive identification of Christ's Mystical Body with the Roman Catholic Church presents
the visible Church in far too eschatological a
fashion; this in turn has led to a keen awareness
of the provisional nature of many structures which
Mystici Corporis had all too hastily carried away
into the eschaton. The Church is *also* the People
of God *on the way*; she may stop at nothing nor
settle anywhere, and her ordinances *ad intra* as
well as her limits *ad extra* are always somewhat
indefinite and sliding. This means that the Church
is also on her way to unity, and she will have to
realize that every fixing of limits and competences
must be provisional, and must never be presented
as identically the same as the eschatological judgment of God, who alone will pronounce the final
"Come, you blessed" and "Depart from me, you curs-
ed." The moment the Church were to rely completely on her limits and ordinances she would harden
in her pilgrim state and thus refuse to submit to
God's final judgment.

This changed self-awareness of the Roman
Catholic Church is, of course, closely related to
her view of other Christian churches. The fact
that Roman Catholic appreciation of other churches
has become so much more positive is, of course,
primarily due to those other Christian churches —
they are so obviously in good faith. [10] Yet the

tium, which did complement and correct *Mystici Corporis*. Cf.
also above, p. 33, note 30.

9. Another very important factor is, of course, the i-
dea, proclaimed at Vatican II with so much gusto by the Orientals, that pluriformity does not stand in the way of unity
— indeed that it enhances it.

10. Obviously it was not just yesterday that the Protestant churches — or the Catholic Church for that matter —
first developed good faith. But is it really an overstate-
ment to say that what good faith there was first had to be
liberated and set free? Was *effective* good faith not wholly conditional on conscious efforts to break the churches'

question whether the Roman Catholic Church would
recognize good faith, not only in Protestants, but
also in Protestant *churches*, was to a large extent
conditioned by the question whether her own self-
concept allowed for such a recognition. Within
the terms of reference of *Mystici Corporis* it was
indeed possible to conceive of Christians in good
faith outside the Church, but it was almost positively excluded that there could be *bona fide* churches. [11]. But ever since the Catholic church has
become more consciously aware of her own pilgrim
state — not excluding the level of unity as willed
and promised by Christ! — , since she has recognized that she is *also on the way* to "the unity of
the faith and the knowledge of the Son of God, to
mature humanity, to the measure of the stature of
the fulness of Christ" (Eph 4, 13), she has also
become more alive to the good faith of other
Christian communities which — like herself, and
given the World Council of Churches, more effect-
ively for the time being — are also on their way
to unity. The essential unity of the Church is no
longer merely conceived of as a "circumscriptive,"
juridically outlined, fixed unity of order; it has
also, and pre-eminently, come to be viewed as
Christ's eschatological gift to his perfect community. It is for this unity that the churches have
to prepare themselves by a growth toward vital, not

own limits, so as to strive for unity in Christ? After all,
"by this people will know that you are my disciples."

11. It remains, of course, possible to say that the
churches "insofar as" they are in good faith are one, and "insofar as" they are under the divisive power of sin are not
one. But that is mincing matters so closely and so ontolog-
ically that the issue at hand, namely, the visible and palpable plurality and division of churches and church orders,
evaporates. In the concrete order, every unity runs the risk
of becoming exclusive. If the churches persevere in an attitude of mutual exclusion there is no good faith. But *bona
fide* churches *can* continually and faithfully try to go beyond their own limits — all limits, that is, that have a
circumscriptive and exclusive nature. Ecumenism, in other
words, is now the concrete shape of the *nota* of Unity.

necessarily uniform, unity among themselves. In
this way, the Roman Catholic view of reunion has
abandoned the retrospective and historical viewpoint, and replaced it by an eschatological and
prospective one. Is it an exaggeration, in light
of Luke 9, 62, to call this development a true
conversion?

Now all churches, whether Catholic, Orthodox
or Reformed, concretize their eschatological perspective, which is the true source of energy and
vital development of any church, in its confession
(creed, deposit of faith, confessional writings)
and its church order. It must be realized, however, that those credal writings and those church
orders, which take shape under the guidance of the
teaching and ruling authorities of the churches,
are ambivalent. On the one hand they render service — they are a form of *diakonia*. On the other
hand they are rules of law, open to the risk of
hardening and sclerosis. Creeds and church orders, which shape the churches' unity of order,
act as the faithful anticipations of eschatological salvation; in this sense they act as a redeem-
ing, saving grace, for they help shape the Kingdom
that is yet imperfect. But if they are to continue
to serve as a form of true *diakonia*, they must
never be allowed to tie salvation down to themselves in a definitive, univocal fashion. Never
must the letter of the profession of faith or of
the church order oppose itself to the pushing
power of the Church, which is always striving for
the full and ultimate revelation of the Kingdom.
In virtue of their very essence they are provisional, capable of truly actualizing salvation only in
an incomplete manner. A church conscious of its
pilgrim state will always realize that the limitations of its creed and church order make it possible, in principle if not in actuality, for the
Kingdom to be concretized along different lines,
and that, as a matter of fact, other churches exist by its side. [12] As long as these churches

_____
12. Difference at the level of creed and church order
can go hand in hand with a strong feeling of kinship at the

do not antagonize each other, but endeavor to arrive at unity in a spirit of obedience to Christ's
word and promise (a unity which may be, but need
not be, found at the level of creed and church order, too), and if they thus go forward through
history towards the eschatological fulfillment
which will ultimately also achieve the promised
unity — as long as all this is the case, creeds
and church orders have an irreplaceable service to
render. If the churches are aware of the fact
that creeds and church orders are essentially related to the eschaton — that is to say, that they
have a relative value — creeds and church orders
will remain alive, open, flexible, and even re-
gaugeable; they will never become an exclusive,
immutable object of faith in themselves. [*13*]

---

level of fundamental attitude; in countries with a strong
ecumenical movement this tends to be increasingly the case.
In parallel fashion, it is possible for credal and institutional unity to coexist with widely divergent funfamental
faith-attitudes; a regular reader of, say, *The National
Catholic Reporter* is liable to feel slightly out of place
in the church in, say, Sicily.

   13. This may need some clarification. The faith-sur-
render to creeds and church orders is never an end in itself. The original sin of the separate churches is argu-
ably their tendency to advance their different creeds and
church orders as *objects* of faith — the *Professio fidei
tridentina* as well as the Heidelberg Catechism or the
Thirty-nine Articles. To put it crudely, this is the typically churchy temptation to ecclesiastical conservatism
on the basis of an exclusive interest in faith and order.
Acceptance of creed and church order must be viewed as the
organon of faith, and the real object of faith would have
to remain, say, "God everything to everyone, through and
beyond death." My acceptance of Jesus as Lord, of my Baptism, of my membership in the Church must act as the organ
of my faith in God, Father, Son, and Holy Spirit. This is
of course no more than an attempt to formulate a principle, to be elaborated also in terms of the hierarchy of
truths. There is obviously an entire range of values between faith in the Lordship of Jesus and acceptance of the
Church's teaching on the effects of the sacrament of the

What has been said so far may be summed up and applied to the problem of the ministry of the sacraments as follows:

1. Baptism, the sacramental acceptance of the divine life by the recognition of Jesus as Lord in the Spirit unites all churches, not only in an eschatological perspective, but already at the level of church order and creed. Baptism, in other words, enjoys inter-church recognition, which means that it is universally valid. [*14*]

2. The ecumenical mentality has created, not just a new political situation among the churches, but also, and primarily, a new theological one, namely the conversion to an eschatological view of the Church, which puts an end to the exclusivist, paradoxical, antithetical situation in which the churches used to antagonize each other. The churches are in good faith, and the differences among the churches no longer bear the stigma of mu-

---

Sick, and between faith in the apostolicity of the Church and adherence to canonical procedural law.

14. It is of paramount importance here to point out that the whole Christian world is thereby also continually tempted to put forward Baptism as an exclusive claim to salvation, pretty much in the same way as Catholics and Orthodox are tempted to narrow down their range of interests to matters of Faith and Order. The entire burden of this chapter should, for that matter, be brought to bear upon the relationship between the churches and the non-Christian world. Why could the reality of salvation not be "fruitfully" at work outside the community of those who have a "valid" Baptism? Cf. John A. T. Robinson's remarks on "current theological radicalism" in *The Honest to God Debate*, London, 1963, p. 250, note 3: "[...] it cuts right across the theological lines, and, like practically every living movement in the Church today, across the ecclesiastical — including that between Rome and the rest. I cannot share the dismay which some have voiced about the damage done to ecumenical relations. It has led to much creative ferment and cross-conversation. And if it prevents a premature closing of the ecclesiastical ranks at the cost of widening the gulf between the Church and the world, it may even be salutary." — Cf. also above, pp. 11, note 1, and 12-13, note 3.

65

tual exclusion, invalidity, and formal heresy.
3. The sacraments are the Church's acts of
faithful worship. They are essentially "sacraments of faith" (*sacramenta fidei*) and "sacraments
of the Church" (*sacramenta ecclesiae*). Just as
the Church actualizes salvation here on earth, in
space and time (*in via*), so do the sacraments:
they are as real and as salutary as the Church that
celebrates them. It is important to note here
that sacraments are essentially anticipatory; if
we should overstate the eschatological nature of
the sacraments we would run the risk of tying salvation down to celebrations that are essentially
provisional, since they are part of the "interim"
situation of the Church, between Jesus' Resurrection and the eschaton. This provisional aspect of
the sacraments is most strongly borne out by the
fact that they are subject to the legal, canonical
qualifications of validity and invalidity.

Thus far we have discussed the first requisite for a true sacrament, which is the milieu in
which it is celebrated, namely, a church in good
faith — where there is Church, there is sacrament. A second question immediately arises, and
it is this: Are these churches, good faith and
all, also in *right* faith in the celebration of
particular sacraments? Is *bona fides* viable without *recta fides* — yes or no? Thus we will have
to turn our attention to the requirements which
the doctrine and the theology implied in the sacraments have to meet. In other words, what is the
function of the deposit of faith, of the credal
statements, of the confessional writings, in the
celebration of the sacraments? It is not till after we discuss this theme that we will be in a position to raise the subject of church order.

The doctrine behind the celebration

Doctrine plays a part in the celebration of sacraments at three different levels: the level of fundamental faith implied in the rite, the level of
orthodox doctrine, and finally the level of theo-

logy. It has already been pointed out [15] that
the Church has always distinguished between these
levels, without always being able, perhaps, to
give adequate reasons for the distinction.

With regard to the third level, sacramental
theology, the Church has always adopted a basic
attitude of great tolerance. The prudential poli-
cies of the Roman curial authorities may indeed,
over the past century or so, have been rather sus-
picious of theological methods which had recourse
to Scripture and patristic tradition rather than
established Roman school theology and magisterial
doctrine; still, no doubt has ever been cast on
anybody's orthodoxy merely on account of his scholarly, theological ideas, as long as they were not
overtly opposed to established doctrine. [16]
The Church's attitude in this respect can be compared with her attitude towards sacramental piety.
Theology has this in common with piety that both
are strongly *a posteriori* and to a high degree determined by circumstances of place and time. Both
arise from faith and doctrine, but both unmistake-
ably bear the marks of situation, taste, thinking
habits, and other background phenomena. Thus, at
a certain point in history the change of the Eucharistic elements was virtually inconceivable except in terms of the Aristotelian categories of
substance and accident; nevertheless, the Council
of Trent did not canonize these categories, and it
showed a healthy sense of relativity with regard
to the term *transsubstantiatio*, by saying no more
than that the term was fitting and to the point. [17]

---

15. Cf. above, p. 41.

16. Is this statement perhaps too optimistic after all?
One sometimes wonders whether the theologians of the Roman
school have not forgotten that they represent a school of
theology, and not the central standard of orthodoxy. This
confusion has led to theological intolerance and, worse
still — in view of the Roman school's closeness to the Roman curial authorities — to ecclesiastical intolerance. To
mention one example, much of the frustrating hassle over the
so-called "Dutch Catechism" has been due to this confusion.

17. In earlier versions of this chapter I made much of

Grounded in Love

Whether a sacrament is a real sacrament is, therefore, dependent on the faith implied in the rite, and in that sense on the acceptance of established doctrine. In technical terms, a sacrament is constituted by the "intention of doing what the Church does," and to that extent by orthodoxy with regard to that particular sacrament. Now we must recall that faith and orthodoxy are not two separate but equal norms in juxtaposition; there is a relationship between them. On the one hand, doctrine is the criterion. If we need to determine whether a person or a group share the Church's fundamental faith with regard to a certain sacrament, and thus, whether he or she or they actually take part in it, we ask the question as to whether these people accept the Church's doctrine on this sacrament in all its essentials. Acceptance of doctrine, or orthodoxy, is consequently used by the governing and teaching authorities in the Church as the publicly acknowledged standard of faith. On the other hand, doctrine is not what makes the sacrament; faith is. The faith implied in the rite — resulting in the intention of doing what the Church does — is the fundamental constitutive factor in the celebration of a sacrament. [18]

---

the fact that Trent speaks in terms of *substantia* and *species* ("appearances"), rather than *substantia* and *accidentia* — thus apparently creating some distance between itself and the Aristotelian categories. E. Schillebeeckx has pointed out, however, that *species* was retained merely because of a tie vote when it was proposed to amend the text to read *accidentia*. It remains true, however, that Trent did not endorse all kinds of technical-scholastic theories about the Eucharistic presence. Cf. on this subject: E. Schillebeeckx, *The Eucharist*, New York, 1968; P. Schoonenberg, "Transubstantiation: How Far is This Doctrine Historically Determined?", *Concilium* 24, pp. 78-91; and James F. McCue, "The Doctrine of Transubstantiation from Berengar through the Council of Trent," in: Paul C. Empie and T. Austin Murphy (eds.), *Lutherans and Catholics in Dialogue, III, The Eucharist as Sacrifice*, Minneapolis, 1967, pp. 89-124.

18. Thus it follows that there is another criterion to determine the value of a sacramental celebration, namely,

Thus, since faith remains at the basis of it all, it can be said to be the "antepredicative" basis of the explicit doctrine. But faith is not just "antepredicative"; it is also "postpredicative" — in the sense that it is faith, not doctrine, that represents the Christian's hopeful surrender to the eschaton. Dogma is partial and provisional; faith is the total surrender of the person to God.

This relationship between fundamental faith and orthodox doctrine is not only relevant with regard to the sacraments, to determine whether in a particular community a particular sacrament is truly celebrated. In other words, the importance of this distinction is not merely that it affords us a handy criterion to judge certain practices with. The relationship is also important in and of itself, because we can extrapolate from it to arrive at a very necessary discussion of a cardinal issue, namely, the relationship betweem faith and the socalled deposit of faith.

The deposit of faith may be said to have two main characteristics. The first is inherent in the deposit of faith as such, whereas the second is of a more factual nature, which is to say that it admits of significant differences according as we are dealing with different items on the long record of orthodox tenets.

Let us start with the second characteristic. Individual doctrinal statements are often antithetical, polemical, apologetical — which amounts to saying they are often incomplete. This is particularly true in the case of the pronouncements made by the Council of Trent with regard to the sacraments. If one compares the sacramental teaching of Trent with, say, the very balanced (and even

---

faithful adherence to the rite, as stated in DS 3874. The difficulty is, of course, that the essential rites of only two sacraments, Baptism and the Eucharist, have been relatively stable over the centuries, so that the Church has had to rely mainly on the standard of orthodoxy with regard to the other sacraments, with their strongly fluctuating rituals. This has had some important consequences, especially in the case of the sacrament of Order.

reasonably ecumenical) Decree on Justification, one cannot but be struck by its polemical tendency, especially in the canons. There is indeed, somewhere in the background of it all, a visible concern to do justice to every aspect of, say, the Eucharist (DS 1635-1661; 1738-1759), but in the actual elaboration so much emphasis is placed on the "objective" aspects of the Eucharist that the essential relationship between the sacrament and the faith of those who celebrate it is given scant attention. [19]

In the heat of the controversy that called for doctrinal pronouncements on particular points the positive clarification conveyed by the pronouncement was, of course, pre-eminent; the Church was, so to speak, relieved at having laid down another solid piece of orthodoxy. But the incompleteness due to the factual history of the pronouncement was not, as such, part of the Church's intention in laying down the doctrine. Many items of orthodoxy, therefore, insofar as they are incomplete, do not as such bind the faithful, nor are they incapable of being completed, amplified, and in that sense corrected.

But what about those doctrinal pronouncements which even at the time when they were formulated were only slightly warped by the need for polemic, because the pope or the council that backed them somehow managed to look beyond the narrow scope of present controversy? What to say about the doctrine of Chalcedon about the two natures in Christ (DS 301-303), or about the above-mentioned Decree on Justification of Trent (DS 1520-1549) — documents so synthetic and balanced that the distortion is minimal? This is where we touch on the first characteristic, the one inherent in the deposit of faith as such, namely, the fact that the

---

19. Note that this is really a matter of emphasis only: "[The Blessed Sacrament] is no less to be adored for having been instituted [...] to be consumed" (*Neque enim ideo minus est adorandum, quod fuit a Christo Domino, ut sumatur, institutum*): DS 1643. Cf. also the expression, "He gave it for them to consume it" (*ut sumerent, tradidit*): DS 1740.

deposit of faith consists of propositional pronouncements made in the past. [20]

We have already explained that the deposit
of faith — especially when purified of onesided
emphases — acts essentially as a *diakonia*, a service rendered to faith; it is the result of the
Church's agelong struggle to actualize and formulate her living faith-experience. Thus orthodoxy
becomes the concrete, palpable shape of salvation
by faith. [21] This is so because the dogmatic
pronouncement does not falsify or distort the original *kerygma*; even the oldest layers of the New
Testament show attemps at theology — the message
intrinsically demands that it be expressed theologically. God's word, after all, is addressed to
thinking human beings, who live in circumstances
of space and time.

Still, in spite of the fact that *kerygma* and
dogma, fundamental faith and orthodox doctrine,
are inseparable, they are not identical. The no-
tional nature of the doctrinal pronouncement (which

---

20. Here the problem of faith and orthodoxy leads to
the fundamental issue of the relationship between *kerygma*
and dogma. Catholic theology, according to Karl Rahner, has
little more than fragments of a theory to offer on this crucial point. Rahner himself makes an attempt at an outline
treatment of the problem in "What is a Dogmatic Statement?"
(*Was ist eine dogmatische Aussage?*), which succeeds in giving an idea of the complexity of the issue (*Theological Investigations* V, London, 1966, pp. 42-66). We have found in
Rahner's attempt many similarities with the general trend of
this chapter; but Rahner does not seem to view the problem
of dogma in an eschatological perspective. Cf. also "Why
Are Dogmatic Pronouncements so Difficult to Make Today?" in:
H. Küng, *The Living Church, Reflections on the Second Vatican Council*, London, 1963, pp. 294-313.

21. Cf. above, pp. 63-64. In the doctrinal pronouncement, the faithful Christian really hears "that original expression of faith itself, not although, but precisely because he hears it in the context of the present Church" (*je-
ne ursprüngliche Glaubensaussage selbst, nicht obwohl, son-
dern gerade weil er sie in Funktion der gegenwärtigen Kirche
hört*): K. Rahner, *Theological Investigations* V, p. 63.

in turn demands some degree of terminological consistency), and especially the fact that the *kerygma* is received and proclaimed by carnal human beings (who are always tempted to use terminological consistency as a handle on faith itself, to get it at their disposal and make it *verfügbar*, as Bultmann would say) — all this causes orthodoxy to be a very ambivalent thing when compared to fundamental faith. The deposit of faith can be a liberating truth, but it can also become a screen, shielding the person against the surrender of faith; and mostly it functions in both ways at the same time. [22] Just as a person's intentions remain the basis of what he expresses in words, doctrine remains based on fundamental faith, "since the latter [*i.e.* the dogmatic statement] must never abandon its original relationship to the kerygmatic faith-expression properly so called." [23]

If doctrine, therefore, is characterized as propositional, this implies that it is the fruit of the apostolic *kerygma*, and also that it must continually be referred back to the living faith-response to the *kerygma*. But both from this fact and from the fact that doctrine was formulated in the past it also follows that it is essentially provisional. Doctrine must also be referred to the future; from the moment it is formulated it is as dependent on continuation (and even correction) as it is on the original experience of faith. Doctrine is *diakonia* to the Church on her way, and may therefore never be allowed to get the Church stuck somewhere in the past. As soon as established doctrine should claim to be the definitive expression of all the truth and all the values faith

---

22. Thus, for instance, the doctrine that the Eucharist is a sacrifice can open our eyes to the deepest meaning of the Eucharist, but also blind us. The latter has been particularly the case whenever the nature of "sacrifice" has been presented as something constant and universal, which has only to be "applied" to the Eucharist.

23. [...] *weil sie ihre Rückbindung zur eigentlichen, kerygmatischen Glaubensaussage nie aufgeben darf*: cf. Karl Rahner, *Theological Investigations* V, p. 58.

represents, it would at once become untrue in a very existential sense. For the deposit of faith is continually being salvaged from becoming untrue by the fact that it is being carried along into the future, and thus going beyond the limitations of the past and taking on new shapes in every new time and circumstance, "until he comes" (1 Cor 11, 26).

Now is this not exactly the awareness that has been developing of late, thanks to the ecumenical movement? The Roman Catholic Church has been maintaining more and more that the deposit of faith is no dead capital, but that it remains vitally related to the living faith-witness, which renews itself as time goes on. Thus, to mention one example, the present consensus on the Eucharist in large parts of the Catholic church far exceeds the doctrines established by Trent. In the Protestant churches, too, there has been a widespread movement to relate their polemical doctrines on the Eucharist (which tended to lay claim to totality of expression) to the integral reality of the Eucharist again. [24] This return, or conversion, to the antepredicative situation, which is at the same time a turning, in hope, to the eschatological fulness beyond all dogma, will enable parties to modify statements made in the past, not necessarily by changing them, but by relating them to the integral experience of salvation. Such conversions may never be branded as "disloyalty to our forefathers," as has been done here and there by integralists and fundamentalists. For what the forefathers were really trying to express — no matter how antithetically and polemically — was no more and no less than their faith. Their formulas were terribly concrete and definite, possibly even to the brink of heresy or beyond it, but the forefathers were the last to want their formulas to become substitutes for faith itself.

The fundamental Christian awareness of salvation by faith remains the fertile soil, the vital

---

24. On this subject, cf. *e.g.*, Leonard Swidler (ed.), *The Eucharist in Ecumenical Dialogue*, New York-Paramus, 1976.

atmosphere, and the true anticipation of our eschatological salvation, also in the celebration of
the sacraments. If a church, in dialogue with
other churches, and basing itself on a radical o-
bedience of faith, is willing to re-consider and
re-gauge its doctrine with regard to certain sacraments, could it perhaps be said that in the case
of such a church any existing doctrinal differences are no longer indicative of "lack of intention
of doing what the Church does"? And might this
not mean that the second condition which every
true sacrament has to meet is met in such a case?

FOUR:

Sacraments and Ministry

WHEN THE profession of faith that was enjoined
upon the Waldensians in 1207 A.D. lists the necessary conditions for the celebration of the Eucharist, it mentions first of all "a certain person,
namely a priest, appointed to precisely that office by a bishop" (*certa persona, id est presbyter
ab episcopo [...] ad illud proprie officium con-
stitutus*). Not until this has been laid down does
the text go on to mention "those solemn words" (*il-
la sollemnia verba*) — the consecration, and hence
the correct rite — and the "right intention of
the person who pronounces them" (*fidelis intentio
proferentis*) — the priest's intention of doing
what the Church does (DS 794). The *Professio* is,
of course, very much a product of its time, but
its very emphatic concern with the minister of the
sacraments is far from being of historical or an-
tiquarian interest only: it looms as large, if not
larger, in theological discussion and debate today. The spadework in sacramental theology done
so ably by theologians like Karl Rahner, Edward
Schillebeeckx and Otto Semmelroth has indeed dis-
posed of the traditional atomistic, hyperclerical
approach to the sacraments, by placing them in
their fundamental context, which is the Church,
the first and original sacrament. But still, concern with the minister is tenacious and (more importantly) of prime ecumenical relevance. A book
like the present one must explore this issue, too.
      We have already pointed out that the invali-
dity of the post-baptismal sacramental celebrations in the churches of the Reformation has always been linked to the Protestant denial of the
sacrament of Order understood as a separate sacra-

75

ment in its own right. [1] Yet, without casting
doubts on the theological and religious honesty of
this argument, the question may well be asked
whether in many cases this has not amounted to taking the path of least resistance. It does not
seem right that many a Catholic theologian can
feel released from the obligation to make a full
and unprejudiced inquiry into the fundamental Protestant attitude of faith with regard to the Lord's
Supper, simply because he can point out that its
ministers don't derive their powers from the Apostolic Succession anyway. This lack of interest in
Protestant faith, predicated on such strong convictions about the futility of the Protestant ministry, has cast a shadow over such controversies
as those between Roman Catholics and High-Church
Anglicans since the beginning of the Oxford Movement. (Not that the issue had not been raised earlier; it very much had, in the controversies between Rome and the Elizabethan and Caroline di-
vines.) The situation was poignant: a large, vo-
cal, and sophisticated group of Catholic believers
had formed in a Protestant church; but all that
was needed, it seemed, to pass a negative verdict
upon the Anglican sacraments as a whole was a declaration that Anglican Orders were invalid. [2]

Thus the question becomes: Are sacraments
tied to ministerial competence, and how, and to
what extent? Is there any maneuvering-room in
Catholic sacramental theology on this score?

---

1. Cf. above, pp. 42-45.
2. This, however, was not only the established theology among Roman Catholics; Anglicans were equally serious on
the subject. The seriousness with which Anglican theologians, especially since the Oxford Movement, and more especially since the reply to *Apostolicae Curae* by the Arch-
bishops of Canterbury aand York, have shown in defending
the validity of Anglican Orders has very often been based
on the same assumption, namely: when matters come to a head,
sacraments depend for their entire validity on the validly
ordained minister. The matter came once again to a crisis
around 1955, when the Anglican Church debated the issue of
intercommunion with the Church of South India; cf. the let-

A summary survey of the history of sacramental practice shows that the validity of the sacraments has never been unequivocally linked up with
the validly ordained minister. In cases of emergency the Church has always had recourse to "extraordinary ministers" (*ministri extraordinarii*).
It is true, present Canon Law has all kinds of
provisions for extraordinary ministers, and sharply delimits their competence; at the same time,
the rise and development of extraordinary ministry
must have been due to the spontaneous faith-instinct
of the faithful (the so-called *sensus fidelium*).
First of all, therefore, we will briefly review
the present position of the ordinary minister, and
then we will review his position in the course of
history. This will enable us, on the basis of
present-day as well as historical fact, to make a
few suggestions, both about the role of canon law
in the Church's sacramental practice and about the
theological implications of the practice of having
extraordinary ministers. After that, we will
briefly summarize our suggestions and apply them
to the problem in hand, namely, the Catholic evaluation of Protestant sacraments in light of their
ministry. Finally, we will try to retrace our
steps, going back from the extraordinary ministry
to the sacrament of Order; this procedure, it is
hoped, will shed some additional light on the ministry in Protestant churches.

---

ter of Walton Hannah, one of the Anglican clergymen who became Catholics over the issue, in *The Month*, N.S. 14(1955)
124-127. In the *Conversations Between the Church of England
and the Methodist Church* (London, 1963), in those passages
which betray an Anglican background (and especially in the
sixth chapter, describing the order of a proposed service of
reconciliation), a lurking preoccupation of the same kind
can be felt; the four authors of "A Dissentient View" in the
same brochure (pp. 57ff.) promptly unmask this reticence
(pp. 59-60). More recent reports of the Committee are
briefly discussed by Henry Chadwick, "The Discussion about
Anglican Orders in Modern Anglican Theology," in: *Concilium*
34, New York - Glen Rock, pp. 141-149.

Some facts

Present-day canon law makes provisions for extraordinary ministers for Baptism and Confirmation
and also, though without using the term, for Marriage. This chapter, it is true, deals only with
the ministry of the post-baptismal sacraments;
still, for the sake of completeness, reference
should be made to the deacon and the lay person
— in some cases even the unbaptized lay person —
acting as the minister of Baptism. [3] With regard to Confirmation, the Code of Canon Law (can.
782 § 2) makes provisions for a priest to administer this sacrament in cases of emergency when a
bishop is not available and in specific territor-
ies; this provision has been considerably broad-
ened since the second Vatican Council. Finally,
the term *minister extraordinarius* could be applied
to an unbaptized person who, after due dispensation, enters upon Matrimony with a baptized Roman
Catholic partner (if, that is, one holds the theological view that this is a true sacrament). The
same could be said of two marriage partners who,

---

3. For a number of stimulating thoughts on Baptism,
which are closely related to the general tenor of the present chapter, cf. E. Schillebeeckx book *Marriage: Secular
Reality and Saving Mystery*, I, London, 1965, pp. 221-238.
Schillebeeckx refers to 1 Cor 7, 14 and to the Jewish custom
of not baptizing children born after their parents' prosel-
yte baptism. The "objective situation of salvation" of fam-
ily solidarity can for good reasons be considered as the *res
sacramenti* of Baptism, so that "birth into a Christian fam-
ily — to two Christian parents — [...][could be] experienced as the sacramental equivalent of baptism. [...] Instead
of forcing these texts to fit the required interpretation,
the study of dogma has in fact far more to gain from trying
to understand more fully the significance of the necessity of
baptism as an incorporation into the community of the church.
In this way it should be possible to learn how to assess theologically those 'frontier' situations which are often capable of revealing in a distinctive and 'flexible' way the real
significance of a requirement posed by dogma." (pp. 233, 235)

in the absence of a priest to witness their Marriage, are within the terms of can. 1098 of the Code
of Canon Law. For the purposes of the present
chapter, however, the extraordinary ministers of
Baptism and Matrimony are (albeit for different
reasons) less important, although they show that
the familiar present-day phenomenon of the extraordinary minister of Confirmation is by no means
an isolated case.

The picture changes when we survey the whole
of sacramental history, for it turns out that the
extraordinary ministry is an age-old practice in
the Church. Church history has extraordinary ministers to show for all the sacraments. Very often
these are extraordinary ministers *de facto*, ante-
cedent to any sort of canonical provisions. Very
often, too, there seem to have been confused (but
very vital) situations that generated a lot of
strife and dispute before any kind of legal security arose. In some cases there may even have been
cases of usurpation, but that does not necessarily
mean that such usurpers, who claimed a particular
sacramental ministry, were devoid of all sacramental sense. However this may be — and we will
come back to this question — this much is certain
that there have been extraordinary ministers for
the Eucharist, the sacrament of Penance, the Anointing of the Sick, and the sacrament of Order. [4]

_____

4. In this chapter we consistently prefer the term
"Sacrament of Order" to "priesthood." First of all, it
seems wrong to call a whole sacrament by the name of merely
its most numerous representatives. Secondly, the term
"priesthood" tends to be associated with a theology of the
sacrament of Order that used to stake its all on the power
of consecration — something that ultimately goes back to
the eucharistic controversies of the early Middle Ages. A-
bove all, however, the term is suspect in view of Scripture,
which emphasizes the priesthood of the entire Church far
more strongly than the priesthood of the Church's ministerial officials. The sacrament of Order is the sacrament of
the service rendered to the Church, and of the Church's hierarchical structure; it bears the mark of priesthood because the Church is also priestly, in her unity with Christ.

In is impossible here to give a complete picture, but what we can do is confirm the statement just made by enumerating a number of eloquent instances of the ministry of the four above-mentioned sacraments being exercised by others than their ordinary ministers.

At the anti-Donatist council of Arles, held in 314 A.D., eleven years before the first ecumenical Council at Nicaea, the following canon was promulgated: "It has come to our notice that deacons offer in many places; we have decreed that this must not happen at all" (*De diaconibus quos cognovimus multis locis offerre, placuit minime fieri debere:* Dz 53; Kirch 373). Without using the term "(in)valid", and so, without passing judgment on what happened in the past, the canon categorically rejects the deacon as the minister of the Eucharist. The power of bishops and priests to preside at the Eucharist is indeed presupposed by the oldest traditions and borne out with special clarity from the fourth century onward. Later on, unequivocal pronouncements of the *magisterium* follow suit: Innocent III (DS 794), the fourth Lateran Council (DS 802) and Clement VIII (DS 1084). But it would appear from the canon of Arles that the Eucharist was *in fact* administered before the year 314, and it seems premature to brand the practice as usurpation (and the sacraments thus celebrated as invalid) if we remember that the canonical rule about the minister of the Eucharist does not turn up in the latest editions of Denzinger-Schönmetzer before the *Professio fidei Waldensibus praescripta* of 1207 A.D. (DS 794). [5]

The ordained priestly ministry, however, no matter how real, represents only one of many forms of hierarchical service.

5. Cf. above, p. 75. — How about references, found in older sources, to "lay people" officiating at the Eucharist, *e.g.*, the prophets mentioned in the *Didache*? References like these do indeed betray a more flexible church order than the church order of, say, the third century onward; still, the risk of reading modern connotations about the distinction between the clergy and the laity into these ancient texts is so great that conclusions are unwarranted.

The history of Penance and its ministers is one of the most elusive and tortuous developments of the first ten or twelve centuries of church history. Eventually it came to be established as a principle that the power to absolve was reserved to the bishop and, to an increasing extent, to the presbyter with jurisdiction from the bishop. But it had taken a long struggle, especially in the East, between the hierarchy and the charismatic monks, to settle the issue. And the fact that the medieval practice of confession to a layman — quite apart from the current theological view that confession of one's sins rather than absolution was the essential part of Penance — was such a wide-spread practice in cases of emergency that a man like Albert the Great could consider it a sacrament, proves that the simple rule which would have only bishops and authorized priests administer the sacrament was anything but a hard and fast one for centuries. [6]

Even the ministry of the Anointing of the Sick, clearly allotted to the "presbyters of the Church" by James 5, 14, has not always been strictly reserved to the priest. The formula of Innocent I in his *rescriptum* to Decentius (DS 216) may indeed leave us in doubt, yet it is certain that quite a number of bishops and ecclesiastical writers between the fifth and eighth centuries, among whom were the Venerable Bede and Caesarius of Arles, did not hesitate in cases of emergency to entrust the Anointing of the Sick to lay people, sometimes with the express motivation that the faithful might otherwise be tempted to resort to local pagan magicians and sorcerers. [7]

---

6. Some particulars taken from *Lexicon für Theologie und Kirche*, under *Laienbeichte*.

7. Some particulars taken from *Lexicon für Theologie und Kirche*, under *Krankensalbung*. — The problem with the text of Innocent I is its doubtful latinity. Innocent quotes James and then goes on: "We must doubtlessly understand this to refer to sick people, who may be anointed with the holy chrism, which, once blessed by the bishop, may be used, not only by (for?) priests, but also by (for?) all Christians

Last, but not least, the sacrament of Order
has known ministers other than ordinary ones,
which provides a rather startling background for
the current and exclusively valid practice of episcopal administration of this sacrament. The most
recent facts in this regard are three fifteenth-
century papal bulls authorizing a few abbots to
ordain deacons, and a few other abbots to ordain
deacons and priests (DS 1145, 1146, 1435). It has
also been established that much earlier, and in a
number of churches, episcopal ordination of bishops
was only gradually introduced. Thus it has been
convincingly argued that Athanasius was the first
patriarch of Alexandria ever to enter upon his office by episcopal laying-on of hands, [8] and there

---

to anoint (to be anointed?) when they, or members of their
households, need it." (*Quod non est dubium de fidelibus ae-
grotantibus accipi vel intelligi debere, qui sancto oleo
chrismatis perungi possunt, quod ab episcopo confectum, non
solum sacerdotibus, sed et omnibus uti Christianis licet in
sua aut in suorum necessitate ungendum.*) After that it is
decided that a bishop can administer the Anointing himself,
and that penitents cannot receive the Anointing, since it is
a sacrament. — The difficulty with the passage is, of course,
whether Innocent wants to say that not only priests but also
lay people may be anointed with chrism, or that lay people
as well as priests can use it to anoint others. An old-time
authority like Cabrol (*Dictionnaire d'Archéologie et de Li-
turgie,* under *Extrême-Onction*) already chose the second interpretation. A survey of all interpretations in E. Doron-
zo, *Tractatus dogmaticus de Extrema Unctione* I, 1954, pp.
116-122.
     8. Thus W. Telfer, "Episcopal Succession in Egypt,"
Journal of Ecclesiastical History 3(1952)1-13. Athanasius'
predecessor Alexander, who played an important role at Nicaea, had been the last to enter upon the office by the old
procedure, which had been aimed at not leaving the See of
turbulent Alexandria empty for as much as one single day.
The "consecration" was effected by the twelve presbyters of
the city appointing one of their own number to the episcopal
office (it is unclear whether this was done by laying-on of
hands or by suffrage) during the funeral ceremonies for the
deceased bishop; they then proceeded to impose the right

are good reasons to assume that episcopal consecration of bishops in the West dates from the days
of Hippolytus and Cyprian, *i.e.*, from the second
half of the second century or the first half of
the third. [9] Still, the most fundamental fact
in this area is the big gap in our information
about the development of the sacrament of Order in
the second century. In spite of the fact that
many ancient sees rightly proved their apostolicity
by referring to their *census*, or list, of bishops,
going back to the apostolic figure responsible for
the foundation of the see, it still remains a difficult task to reconstruct the link between the
loosely organized but clearly existent leadership
of the New Testament communities and the established hierarchy of bishops, priests and deacons of
the third century. [10] Historically speaking, the
results of the search for the missing link have
been meagre, no matter how pertinent the search.
But it may be asked whether the gap itself, namely
the lack of any detailed and definite information
about an established hierarchical order, must not

---

hand of the dead bishop on the head of the bishop-elect.
Telfer concludes his careful historical analysis as follows:
"In the days of Nicaea, the keystone of apostolic ministry
was not held to be a particular rite for the making of a
bishop. There was no general belief that valid episcopal
succession was inseparable from an unbroken chain of consecration by laying on of hands. [...] The tyranny of legalism
was still at bay." (12)

9. Cf. N. Sykes, *Old Priest and New Presbyter*, Cambridge, 1956, pp. 239-240.

10. A classical and very fine effort was made by the
Anglican Benedictine Dom Gregory Dix, in "The Ministry in
the Early Church," in: Kenneth E. Kirk (ed.), *The Apostolic
Ministry*, Oxford, 1946, pp. 183-303. However, it seems that
in his eagerness to assert the validity of Anglican orders
by means of the idea of "historic episcopate", Dix insists
on tracing a sort of "essence" of the episcopal office
right through the dark second century, with the result that
he arrives at little more than a most interesting hypothesis. — Substantially new progress has been made in this a-
rea of research by Jean Colson's numerous publications.

be turned into a *positive* theological argument.
There was leadership, hierarchy, order in the New
Testament, and there was hierarchy in the third
century; the basic pattern of the latter has become the canonically established hierarchical pattern today. This proves at least that a principle
of order, embodied in specially appointed persons,
existed and was continued throughout the second
century. At every stage this *Ordo* functioned as
the governing agency of individual communities and
as the bond of unity among communities. However,
for all the continuity, it would be premature to
say, for example, that the "power of consecration"
always was the "privilege" of the "bishops"; if we
were to say that, we would be talking about the
second century in terms of the third.

The origin of law; its function
in normal and paradoxical situations

So far we have established that all sacraments have
in the course of history been administered by ministers other than ordinary ones. The question now
arises how to account for the facts theologically.
We must, however, start with a distinction. Although we have thus far applied the term *minister*
extraordinarius to all non-ordinary ministers in-
discriminately, we should remind ourselves that
the extraordinary minister in the juridical and
technical sense of the word is a far cry from the
minister who volunteers in an emergency. In concrete terms, the pastor who administers Confirmation or the lay person who baptizes is an extraordinary minister in a sense different from the
deacons in the South of Gaul before the council
of Arles told them to stop celebrating the Eucharist, or the comrade-in-arms to whom Ignatius
Loyola made his lay confession on the ramparts
of Pampeluna in 1521. The former are canonically
recognized ministers, whose ministry is guaranteed by the Church in specific cases; the latter
may indeed derive their ministry from somewhere,
but they are — or were — certainly not recog-

nized by canon law.

Let us attempt to clarify the difference by investigating the background of the canon of Arles and venturing an interpretation. During the persecution of Diocletian (303-311 A.D.) the harried Christians had been forced to celebrate the Eucharist in secret, and they had for that purpose called upon deacons to officiate when the bishops or the presbyters were not available. [11] Now it seems that after the establishment of religious freedom by the Edict of Milan in 313 A.D. there were deacons who went on exercizing, and perhaps even claiming, a ministry for which they had only deputized in an emergency situation. In that case the canon of Arles is not a re-enforcement of a rule of law which had been in force and known to be in force, and which in an emergency situation had been pardonably though wrongly broken. Rather, the canon is a piece of original codification, which now lays down as a rule of law a practice which must have been self-evident under normal circumstances, namely, that only bishops and au-

---

11. Cf. the very summary discussion of the facts in Hefele, *Histoire des Conciles* I, 1, Paris, 1907, pp. 291-292. — For the sake of completeness, two other interpretations of the canon of Arles should be mentioned here. The first suggests that "offer" (*offerre*) here refers to the cult of idols during the persecution; the second maintains that the canon means the same as canon XVIII of the Council of Nicaea, namely, that in the presence of bishops or priests deacons do not enjoy precedence in administering or receiving the Eucharist, since theirs is a subordinate function in the liturgy. Both interpretations, however, seem to strain the text, and are apparently aimed at precluding the possibility of an extraordinary ministry of the Eucharist. — As for the authorities behind Dz, the following remarks are appropriate. Dz cites Mansi II, 469ff.; Mansi cites Nicaea, Jerome, Epiphanius and Urban VIII. Nicaea's canon XVIII has a different question in mind, as we have just seen. Neither Jerome nor Epiphanius really discuss the question in hand; they just touch on it and cannot, therefore, be alleged as real witnesses. Urban VIII is too late (12th century) to be of any relevance to the question.

Grounded in Love

thorized priests are the ministers of the Eucharist.
        Let us try to state the matter in general
terms. The normal, generally accepted practice is
for the community to avail themselves gratefully
of the services of its authoritative "diaconic"
officials, whose ministry makes it possible for
the church community to take shape in an orderly
fashion. On the basis of this practice, and
most of all, in view of abuses or disputes about
matters of competence, the Church gradually devel-
ops a body of rules of law, which regulate the
ministry of the sacraments — ministry becomes a
matter, not only of authoritative *diaconia*, but
also of lawful exercise of power. In doing so,
the Church reserves the ministry of each individual sacrament to specific "ordinary" ministers.
And so it is that a body of canon law arises.
This body of canon law functions differently according as situations differ.
        It does not function at all, in the sense
that it does not act as a separate, extra factor,
in normal circumstances, in which the community
spontaneously turns to its ministerial officials
for the ministry of the sacraments. In saying
this we are only re-stating a remark made in a
previous chapter: the validity of a sacrament
does not normally play a part in the awareness of
those who celebrate it. [12] If one were to insist on attributing some role to legal rules under
normal circumstances, it could be argued that in
such cases the rule acts as an implicit check on the
ecclesial loyalty — in Ignatian terms, the *senti-
re cum ecclesia* — of the *bona fide* community of
the faithful.
        The rule of law — and with it, the concept
of validity — comes into immediate action in the
paradoxical situation, which arises when a non-au-
thorized minister presumes to administer the sacrament under normal circumstances. [13] Something

_____
    12. Cf. above, pp. 46-47.
    13. To clarify our terminology: A situation is called
"paradoxical" when there prevails an antithesis between the

86

should be pointed out here right away. In making her recognition, and hence the validity, of a sacrament dependent upon the adherence to a body of canon law regulating the ministry of this particular sacrament, the Church is making this sacrament not directly, but only indirectly dependent upon legal requirements. It is indeed true that a person who thus goes against the law does not celebrate the sacrament, because he flouts the "power of the keys" (*claves ecclesiae* — DS 802). It is not that he does not want to, or is unable to, celebrate the sacrament; rather, he is going against the canonically established church order, and thus he is presumed to go against the Church and her intentions, to the extent that the Church has made the endorsement of her intentions dependent on adherence to the church order. [*14*]

---

intentions (actions) of the minister (recipient) and those of the Church; thus, paradoxical situations are those in which bad faith plays a role, so that the sacrament becomes invalid or. at least unfruitful (leaving the paradox of the *bona fide* celebration of an objectively invalid sacrament [cf. above, p. 47] aside for the moment). This paradoxical situation must be distinguished from the extraordinary situation, in which, by definition, there is good faith, but in which the community that celebrates the sacrament finds itself in an emergency situation owing to the fact that the normal ecclesiastical institutions are upset.

    14. Cf. DS 794 (*Professio fidei Waldensibus praescripta* — cf. above, pp. 75, 80): "[...] and therefore we steadfastly believe and profess that whoever believes *and maintains* [author's emphasis] that he or she is capable of effecting the Eucharistic sacrifice without benefit of antecedent episcopal ordination, as we have pointed out, is a heretic [...] (*[...] ideoque firmiter credimus et confitemur, quod quicumque sine praecedenti ordinatione episcopali, ut praediximus, credit* et contendit *se posse sacrificium Eucharistiae facere, haereticus est [...]*). — Traditional theology, with its strong emphasis on validity, has tended to equate rather too easily God's eschatological judgment with the black-and-white situation which the dependence of a sacrament on a canonical system tends to create. But there is a difference. The body of canon law is a typically juri-

The extraordinary situation:
basis of the extraordinary ministry

How does the law function in extraordinary situations? We would like to suggest that it loses its
binding force: "necessity has no law." How can
this be? A rule of law is never meant to replace
the fullness of real life or to render it super-
fluous; it merely regulates and channels it. Under
all circumstances the rule of law remains based on
the full ante-juridical reality, which the law
does no more than tighten up and clarify in the
interest of the common good. If, therefore, we
say that necessity knows no law, this is not to
say that anarchy is the only alternative to legal
order. Rather, the emergency situation lays bare
the hidden but powerful resources of life which
are the hidden foundation of the legal system, and
which continue to support and undergird the legal
system even when it does apply. [15] In an emergency it suddenly becomes clear that this hidden
foundation harbors an "order of love" — an *ordo
caritatis* — , a fullness of life and a flexibility which the rule of law might often seem to
have completely obliterated.

Let us apply this theory to our problem. In
cases of emergency, we suggest, the absence of an
authorized minister turned out not to be an obstacle to the celebration of the sacrament; if
and when necessary the extraordinary minister —
someone with no canonical credentials — emerged
to deputize. Whether this was valid or not was no

---

dical simplification of ecclesial reality, which in itself
comprises much more than canonical absolutes. It is indeed
true that the attitude of the faithful in regard to the Church
is an anticipation of God's eschatological judgment, but
this attitude is one of hopeful surrender in the dark light
of faith; this vitally obscure faith-attitude will eventually have to pass under God's judgment — just like the Church
as a whole, for that matter. Cf. above, pp. 29-30, esp. note 23.

15. The idea expressed here lies at the basis of the
whole of this book; cf. above, pp. 2-4.

issue at all, for those who gathered to celebrate
the sacrament were in more than good faith, especially under the stress of the emergency. And
it was felt to be less relevant under the circumstances to make sure that the church authorities
would approve or recognize the celebration: *prius
vivere, dein philosophari* — start by living, and
then think about it!

With the incorrigible optimism of the legis-
lator, who hopes eventually to provide for all
situations and prevent evil and abuse in all situations, [16] the leadership in the Church set
out to make juridical provisions for emergency
situations, too. The *minister extraordinarius* in
the technical sense of the term was the result of
this effort. But here a question arises. What
is it, theologically (not juridically!) speaking,
that entitles the extraordinary minister to claim
that his ministry is truly sacramental? It cannot be diaconic *and* canonical qualification, which
is the sole title of the ordinary minister; therefore it can only be the diaconic ministry itself,
plus the fact that the Church recognizes this ministry in advance as authentic under circumstances
of emergency. It is important to be very clear at
this point. Theologically speaking, it has always
been a crux to explain why in cases of emergency,
in the absence of a bishop, a priest could suddenly administer Confirmation, [17] or why the ab-

---

16. For it must indeed be admitted that in the extraordinary situation, if one goes only by the objective events,
it is very difficult to determine whether the celebration
is done in good faith or not. It takes participation to know.

17. An analogous question could be asked about Baptism
administered by a non-baptized person. — This may be expanded. The sacrament of Order comprises much more than
just the power of consecration; the authoritative exercise
of ecclesiastical jurisdiction (often considered a secondary qualification of the ordained minister) is equally important. Now it appears that the Church also knows "extraordinary jurisdiction." In imminent danger of death or similar situations (the classical example used to be the man
about to be deported to Siberia) every priest suddenly has

bots of St. Osyth in England, Altzelle in Saxony,
and Citeaux in Burgundy along with its daughter
abbeys, upon receipt of a papal bull, could suddenly ordain deacons and priests. It looks very
improbable that the reality of a sacrament can be
adequately accounted for by recourse to an authorization of so strongly legal a nature. Law of
its essence is not creative — it regulates reality. Canonical recognition of a sacrament is not
the same as the sacrament itself, and advance recognition as a means for providing for special
cases remains a recognition and no more. The
true origin of the sacrament in these cases,
therefore, has to be found *in the situation itself*; [18] the local community of Christian faith-

---

full faculties, not only to absolve, but also to grant dis-
pensations in a number of marriage impediments. The practice of *sanatio in radice* ("healing in the root") points in
a similar direction. *Sanatio* is a non-sacramental procedure by which a marriage is declared valid retroactively,
from the moment true marital consent came about; this makes
theological sense only if it is assumed that there was something prior to the *sanatio*. Could this "something" be a
true, sacramental, although extraordinary Marriage, whose
validity is only established at a later moment? Summing up,
all these extraordinary events again go to show that the
Church does not tie salvation down to a strictly legal canonical order. Cf. above, pp. 63-64, esp. also note 13.

    18. This is not a dogmatic variety of situation eth-
ics. After all, being situated is an essential factor in
human nature, and not merely an extrinsic determinant. The
Church herself could, in relation to every individual
Christian, be described in terms of the concept of "situation." It follows that I must disagree with Tavard when he
renders the tentative solutions proposed by Hans Küng and
myself as follows: "[...] if the empirical community he
[the baptized person] belongs to has no regular episcopal
succession to provide an orderly Eucharist, his baptism
will suffice to supply what may be wanted in the ministry
of his church. Or, which amounts to the same, a minister
who has received no more than baptism has received enough
to provide the Eucharist to the fellow members of his community" ("Does the Protestant Ministry Have Sacramental

ful, in virtue of Christ's presence, can celebrate his saving presence in a sacramental way. The rule of law recognizes this possibility in advance, as long as the community's action does not go against the existing church order, but merely "bypasses" it — extraordinary ministry is not *contra ordinem*, but *praeter ordinem*. In emergencies this possibility becomes an actuality: the community calls upon its pastor, or its abbot, to act as the minister presiding over the celebration of Confirmation or Holy Orders. The priest, who under normal circumstances would offend against the church order (and thus would be presumed to act against the intentions of the Church, thereby frustrating the sacrament), deputizes with the intention of doing what the Church ordinarily does through the ministry of the bishop. [19] The authenticity of this ministry is recognized in advance, and therefore the sacrament is valid. The *opus operatum*, which really is "the work of Christ who is active in the

---

Significance?", *Continuum* 6(1968)260–269, quotation 262). To call a Protestant church an "empirical" community is to disregard its share of *ecclesial* reality, which is precisely the *situation*, in the existential sense of that word, which lifts the extraordinary minister above his *individual* status of one "who has received no more than baptism." Do I detect in Tavard's words some of the traditional individualist approach to sacramental reality? — Cf. Tertullian, who reminds his readers "that the difference between *ordo* and *plebs* (clergy and people) does not go back to Christ and the apostles, adding, "are we laymen not also priests? Where three, even if they are laymen, are gathered together, there the Church is'." (*De Exhort. Cast.*, 7, 3; quoted in Joseph Blenkinsopp, "Presbyter to Priest: Ministry in the Early Church," *Worship* 41(1967)428–438, quotation 431.)

19. Cf. the following example of a formula expressing ordinary ministry (DS 1741): "Jesus Christ instituted the new Pasch, giving himself to be sacrificed under visible signs *by the Church through priests* [author's emphasis] in memory of his going from this world to the Father" (*Jesus Christus novum instituit Pascha, seipsum ab Ecclesia per sacerdotes sub signis visibilibus immolandum in memoriam transitus sui ex hoc mundo ad Patrem*).

Church" (*opus operantis Christi in Ecclesia*), is stronger than the church order established for normal situations.

The trouble is, of course, that the law can never provide for all situations, even if provisions for the most frequently occurring emergencies have been incorporated into the legal system by means of the advance assignment of extraordinary ministers. [20] When a group of Christians gets somewhat isolated from the normal, ordinary life of the Church, without the prospect of a speedy normalization of its legal status, it may be asked whether in such a situation the rule of

---

20. Is it proper here to appeal to the traditional doctrine that only Baptism is necessary for salvation in the strict sense of the word, and that an isolated group of Christians can therefore safely dispense with the other sacraments (except Matrimony: Code of Canon Law, can. 1098)? Perhaps it is. Yet, the question as to whether a sacrament is necessary for salvation is based on a conception of the sacraments which — although not wrong — is at least very incomplete, and maybe even fails to appreciate the essence of a sacrament. Only a means can be said to be more or less necessary in order to attain a certain end. The question, therefore, makes sense only if the sacraments are to be viewed as the (minimal?) means to salvation, put at the disposal of the (individual?) faithful by the Church (viewed as an extrinsic and clerical agency?). But if the sacraments are in the first place celebrations of a community, then the question plays a subordinate role. Somebody who would first of all want to decide whether a birthday party is necessary for him to lead a happy life would disregard the very nature of the celebration. Meanwhile, however, it is obvious that the thesis that the post-baptismal sacraments are not necessary for salvation is not meaningless. Unforeseen circumstances, such as the absence of an ordinary minister or a canonically qualified extraordinary minister, do not in fact create an emergency situation in each individual case; in other words, the post-baptismal sacraments are not necessary for salvation *in particular cases*. The impossibility for one or more sacraments to be administered in individual cases is, therefore, not an extraordinary situation, but part of the normal human predicament of the Church.

law does not drop out as the standard of sacramental activity altogether. The ante-juridical,
vital foundations of law, on which the legal system had continued to rely even while it did apply,
are now laid bare. In this hypothesis the isolated "little Church" (*Ecclesiola*), in virtue of
Christ's presence, could celebrate her sacraments,
administered by those who in this particular congregation take the burden of ministry upon themselves in view of their spontaneous and recognized
ability to serve as leaders. In such cases, we
suggest, the community could claim a truly sacramental character for these celebrations on the
strength of the diaconic nature of the ministry
itself plus the possibility for this ministry to be
recognized as authentic. In more traditional
terms, the theological basis of the authenticity
of the extraordinary ministry seems to be the common (in the sense of communal!) priesthood of the
faithful, which under normal circumstances oper-
ates through the persons of the recognized, ordained ministers, and which in cases of emergency
is exercized through the ministry of those who deputize.

It is indeed true that to our knowledge the
sacraments of Confirmation, Eucharist, and Holy
Orders have never been administered by lay people.
[21] Yet we venture to suggest that the principle

---

21. Cf. above, p. 86, note 5. — Anglican theology,
traditionally loyal to continental Protestants as much as to
the episcopal church order, may well be able to make some
valuable contributions on this point. The high-church theologians of the sixteenth and seventeenth centuries recognized the ministry of the presbyterian churches on the con-
tinent in view of the state of emergency prevailing there.
For example, Protestant bishops in France were an impossibility, because episcopacy could only exist where a "godly
Prince" was willing and able to protect it. "Accordingly
Hall's conclusion that episcopacy 'for the main substance is
now utterly indispensable, and must continue to the world's
end,' was qualified by the explanation: 'indispensable by
any voluntary act; what inevitable necessity may do in such
a case, we now dispute not; necessity hath dispensed with

just elaborated, added to the fact that the sacraments of Penance and Anointing of the Sick have
been administered by lay people, lends sufficient
support to our hypothesis that a protracted absence of canonically qualified ministers throws
the community back upon itself for the celebration
of its sacraments, and that it can do so by making
use of the services of those among its members
who spontaneously take the lead, and whose leadership is recognized by the community. All of this
would be based on Baptism, of which the sacramental ministry is the ultimate ministerial concretization and shape; ministry in the Church is a very
pointed version of the general call to service implied in Baptism. [22]

At this point it seems useful to deal with an
ambiguity which George H. Tavard has pointed out
in a critical discussion of the previously published versions of the present chapter, and of a
similar suggestion made by Hans Küng. [23] Tavard
writes: "To these two approaches I oppose a fundamental objection: in both cases, the entire burden of introduction into Christianity has been
placed on baptism. It is from baptism and its
consequence, the participation of all the faithful
in the one priesthood of Christ through the so-
called universal priesthood of believers, that van
Beeck and Küng deduce the empowerment of the faithful to act as leaders of the Eucharistic action.
The person who has been baptized has a right and a
duty to share in the Lord's Supper; whence it follows that, if the empirical community he belongs
to has no regular episcopal succession to provide

---

some, immediately divine laws. Where then that may be just-
ly pleaded, we shall not be wanting both in our pity and in
our prayers'." (N. Sykes, *Old Priest and New Presbyter*, p. 75.

22. Although we are specifically dealing here with the
sacraments we do not by any means wish to exclude the authoritative ministry of the Word. Through Baptism the Word has
been entrusted to the community; the ministry of the Word in
the community in extraordinary circumstances is authentic on
the strength of the *diakonia* itself.

23. *E.g.* in his *The Church*, esp. section E, I, 2 and II, 2.

an orderly Eucharist, his baptism will suffice to
supply to what may be wanting in the ministry of
his church. Or, which amounts to the same, a minister who has received no more than baptism has
received enough to provide the Eucharist to the
fellow members of his community."
Tavard them goes on to articulate his two
principal objections.
1. "This attribution to baptism of all the
modalities and capacities of Christian life and
organization is tantamount to a fantastic reduction of a much more complex reality." Baptism is
only the first initiation, and it grants "no
right to the Eucharist and no power other than the
spiritual power to further initiation. One cannot, in this perspective, reduce the post-baptismal sacraments to an 'intensification and specification of baptism.' [24] Baptism does not 'include'
the other sacraments; it is not an 'overflowing
source,' but it has itself to be enriched by what
follows, especially the gift of the Spirit and the
Eucharistic banquet." To what Tavard perceives as
a "baptism-centered conception of christian life,"
implying an "unrealistic and unacceptable sacramental reductionism," he opposes a "Eucharist-centered" conception, which he claims has the support
of the patristic and medieval tradition.
2. "The functional priesthood of the minister
is in the views of van Beeck and of Hans Küng, related to the general priesthood of the faithful by
way of implication. The ministry is contained in
the general priesthood [...] Now, my understanding
of ministry does not admit of the categories of implication in the universal priesthood, or of mere
representation of the community. For, once again,
the medieval and patristic models point in another
direction: the ministry depends on a charism given
for the sake of the community, and which the community shares only to the extent that it recognizes some of its members as having this gift. The
functional eucharistic priesthood cannot be sub-

---

24. Tavard here uses an expression we will use below,
p.122, and which also occurred in our previous publications.

sumed under the universal priesthood of the faithful. No reduction of the one to the other is possible if we want to do justice to the patristic
and medieval tradition." [25]

Anyone even slightly familiar with classical
sacramental theology and ecclesiology, and — more
importantly — with the prevailing sensibility of
large numbers of Christians on both sides of the
ecumenical fences, will recognize the importance
of the questions raised by Tavard. Yet, precisely
because they are part and parcel of classical theology they may prove very helpful in framing the
tentative answers this chapter is trying to discover.

First of all, far from reducing sacramental
reality to Baptism, or making Baptism the center
of the Christian life, the solution proposed in
this chapter is precisely conceived in the interest of a Eucharist-centered view of the Christian
life. Why otherwise bother about the status of
the post-baptismal sacraments in the churches of
the Reformation?

Secondly, this Eucharist-centered view of the

---

25. George H. Tavard, "Does the Protestant Ministry
Have Sacramental Significance?", *Continuum* 6(1968)260-269,
quotations 262-263. — In all honesty I must say that Tavard's rendering of Küng's views and mine, while inspired by
a legitimate theological concern, is inadequate and quite
tendentious, which appears from some expressions. My definition of extraordinary ministry is not correctly rendered by
"improperly installed but *validly* functioning" (my italics);
in fact, I have consistently avoided the word "valid" in
this connection, and used "recognizable" instead. To suggest that for Küng the general priesthood is "the only *hier-
archia*" is to do him an injustice — to my knowledge he never uses the word in the passages referred to. And to state
that Küng's view, and mine, of the functional priesthood
"comes near to the Protestant conception of the ministry" in
that it uses the category of "mere representation," is unfair if such a statement is not accompanied by references to
elaborate discussions of the Catholic conception of ministry,
both in Küng's writings and in the previously published versions of the present chapter.

Christian life is expressed in terms of that reality of which the Eucharist is at once the seal and
the creative force: the Church. In other words,
the *ecclesial* character of the hypothetical group
of baptized Christians adds up to more than the
sum of the sacramental qualifications of the individual baptized Christians. Küng has correctly
pointed out that it is not the extraordinary situation or the emergency situation taken by itself
(*i.e.*, viewed as a particular *legal* predicament),
but the abiding possibility for the Spirit to act
in the faithful through *charismata*, [26] which
warrants our hypothesis. Put in the terminology
of this book, what warrants the extraordinary ministry is the work of Christ who is active in the
Church — *opus operantis Christi in Ecclesia.*

   Thirdly: Tavard, therefore, is asking a very
important question when he writes: "My question to
a Protestant minister is therefore the following:
in what way do you function. Do you believe your-
self to function, and are you recognized by your
community as functioning, as a eucharistic priest?
If the priestly language still occasions difficulties, as it did at the Reformation, I will say: Do
you belong to a eucharistic community in which you
function as the president of the Supper? Are you
known by your people as the one whose central task
is to lead the faithful into eucharistic communion?" [27] What Küng has attempted to discover,
and what this chapter is trying to explore, is the
answer to two further questions, namely (1) *In
virtue of what* does the community recognize the
minister of the Eucharist?, and (2) *In virtue of
what* does such a minister recognize the community's
recognition of himself, and accept its acceptance
of himself?

   The answer to these questions is *not*: Because
any member of the faithful is *empowered*, or can
claim to be entitled, to act as the leader of the
Eucharistic action, or because someone "who has
received no more than baptism has received enough

----

26. H. Küng, *The Church*, esp. section E, I, 2.
27. G. Tavard, *op. cit.* 266-267.

to provide the eucharist to the fellow members of his community." Such an answer would indeed make the Baptism of an *individual* into the "overflowing source" of all kinds of sacramental powers, most of which would, in the normal situation, happen to be "frozen", so to speak, in the style of a kind of *potestas ligata* (a power someone has, but which he is not free to use). In that same frame of reference, the other sacraments would indeed be "implied" or "included" in Baptism — something Tavard rightly finds unacceptable.

The correct answer, therefore, is quite different, and it would seem to run as follows. The common Baptism is no more (but also: no less) than the *basis* upon which further sacramental activity could *develop, grow, and flourish* in the midst of the ecclesial community. Tavard points in the same direction when he says that "the eucharistic validity of the ministry could, as it were, revive and resurrect," provided "the conformity of a given eucharistic doctrine with the Catholic tradition" were to be ascertained. [28]

After what we have proposed, we would like to summarize our hypothesis as follows. For a rite to be a true sacrament if administered by a baptized Christian who does not stand in the Apostolic Succession (but who does stand in the Apostolic Tradition) it is required that, besides ecclesial

---

28. G. Tavard, *op. cit.* 267. — There remains, of course, the question of the thought models which I think I discover in the way in which Tavard poses the problem. It can be summarized, as I see it, in two questions. 1. Is it possible to conceive of something really new (= the post-baptismal sacraments) and vitally connected with the old (= Baptism), and yet not as merely implied in the old, or dependent on the old as an effect is dependent on a cause? 2. Is it possible to conceive of a new qualification (= the ministry of the post-baptismal sacraments) in terms other than either "mere representation" or a property added on "from the outside"? My answer would be affirmative in both cases, and I would, by way of quick suggestion, point to an evolutionist conception of causality with a strong stress on divine concurrence, and to a corporate concept of community.

background and intention of doing what the Church does, [29] there be found good faith and a protracted extraordinary situation. The latter makes it possible for the sacraments to be administered "church order aside" (*praeter ordinem*), whereas the former sees to it that what is being done is not in fact "against the church order" (*contra ordinem*), and thus, as may be presumed, "against the Church" (*contra Ecclesiam*). [30] In spite of ecumenism, the churches of the Reformation are not subject to the church order of the Roman Catholic Church; at the same time, their ecumenism bears witness to the fact that they no longer intend to celebrate the sacraments in an antithetical spirit. [31] Thus we are in a position to finally formulate our hypothesis: in view of the extraor-

---

29. For the doctrinal acpects of this, cf. above, pp. 66-74.

30. Should this hypothesis hold good, then it would be acceptable for a group of Christian lay people serving life sentences in a concentration camp to celebrate the Eucharist without adherence to the normal church order, which reserves this ministry to the ordained minister. We suggest that under such circumstances the validity of the rite should not be questioned; in our hypothesis the *opus operatum* (or rather, the work of Christ who is at work in the Church) guarantees the authenticity of the celebration, which is indeed not valid in the technical sense, but at least *recognizable*. This hypothesis might look for support from the permission allegedly given by Pope Pius XII in 1940-1945, to celebrate the Eucharist in concentration camps with bread only; such an indult would go much further than a mere exception to the church order! Cf. also Joseph Duss-von Werdt, "What Can the Layman Do without the Priest?", in: *Concilium* 34, New York - Glen Rock, 1968, pp. 105-114.

31. *In concreto:* when the Lord's Supper is celebrated in a Protestant church today, there is no intention of celebrating an "anti-Mass." We leave aside the question whether this has ever been the case, and if so, when this attitude of (mutual!) exclusion began to yield to mutual good faith. That is something to be historically investigated by others. Here we are trying to concentrate on the prospective orientation of the search for unity — cf. above, pp. 60-66.

99

dinary situation, the good faith, and the authenticity of the ministry, supported by the faith and
the ecclesial character of the community, the ministry of (the Word and) the sacraments as exercized by Protestant ministers may be qualified, in
the framework of the Roman Catholic church order,
as *recognizable as extraordinary ministry.*

The essence of the sacrament of Order and its canonical shape

If our efforts have led to a satisfactory result
so far, we may not foster any illusions. We must
quickly remind ourselves of the fact that in most
Protestant churches the situation is certainly not
such that — in the absence of ordinary ministers
— regular members of the community deputize in
the ministry of the Word and the sacraments. The
Protestant churches have always had church orders
of their own and specifically appointed ministers,
for whom it would be poor comfort indeed to see
themselves recognized by Roman Catholics as extraordinary ministers, and therefore equivalently as
lay people. The question, therefore, (the actual,
practical ministry of the sacraments aside) is one
of principle, too, and it runs: can the sacrament
of Order be said to be present in Protestant
churches? Is the presence of a body of ministers
as laid down in the church order not precisely the
presence of the sacrament of Order? Or are we to
say that all the sacraments, except (by definition) the sacrament of Order, admit of extraordinary ministers? In other words, is the Apostolic
Succession the only channel through which the sacrament of Order is continued in the Church? [32]

---

32. Ecumenically speaking, this question is of the
greatest moment. Is it sufficient for intercommunion and
communion for other churches to "take episcopacy into their
own system" (Archbishop Geoffrey Fisher's famous speech to
the University of Cambridge in 1946), the way it happened
in the formation of the Church of South India, or must all
ministers of non-episcopal churches and all (successors of)
invalidly ordained ministers of episcopal churches be (re)-

To put the alternative in brief words: Can only
the *sacraments* administered by Protestant ministers be recognized, or can their *ministry as such*
be recognized also?

Our thesis is going to be that there are good
reasons for an affirmative answer to the second
half of our dilemma. We shall do this in four
steps. After a few preliminary remarks of a more
negative nature we will describe the relationship
between Church and ordained ministry or *Ordo*. After that, we will have to do justice to the teaching of the Church about the difference between ordination and delegation, and to the question about
the nature of Apostolic Succession. This will
prepare us for our conclusions.

Some preliminaries

Let us lay down from the outset that ministry and
laity are not two irreducible levels in the Church.
As early as the New Testament there is indeed a
clear awareness of the distinction between the authorities and the community; Paul's letters, the
Pastorals and Acts bear witness to this fact on
almost every page. But it should be pointed out at
once, too, that the origin and the continuation of
the Church is not only based on the authoritative
preaching of the Gospel, but also on the inspired
response which the preaching evokes in and among
those who believe (cf., *e.g.*, 1 Thes 1-2). At the
same time, the New Testament shows efforts at clarifying the existence of different degrees of initiation into the mystery of the Kingdom, corres-
ponding to different functions in the preaching of
the Gospel. The synoptic distinction between the
masses and the Twelve, for instance, bears witness
to distinctions in the early Church (no matter how
hard it may be to decide in the case of each particular saying to whom it was first addressed). The
exact definition of the distinction, however, may
often have been a matter of doubt, as is illustrated by Luke 12, 41: "Peter said, Lord, are you

ordained by Catholic, Orthodox, or Old Catholic bishops?

Grounded in Love

telling this parable for us or for all?"

Yet, for all the emphasis on the distinction, the total impression is one of unity. The New Testament itself is a case in point: the whole body of writings — including the Pauline letters to some extent — is the result of a harmonious, organic collaboration between the communities of believers and the leadership of the eye-witnesses, the apostles, and their immediate associates. Nowhere does it look as if Christ founded the Church on two separate, irreducible levels; the responsible ministry is too organically incorporated into the life of the communities for the two to be mutually exclusive and irreducible.

We can argue this in a more speculative way, too. If there were two separate levels in the Church, this would ultimately lead to two "churches". An apt illustration of this tendency is actually the clericalism of the Latin church with its striking identification, down to the level of everyday speech, of "Church" and "clergy" ("a churchman", "go into the church", "the church teaches"). Overcoming a heritage of clericalism is not the least task the Catholic Church after Vatican II is seeking to accomplish, and the difficulty we are having in developing a theology of the laity is not in the last place due to this clericalism, with its strongly legal, canonical roots. The black-and-white definitions of the legal mind (either you are ordained or you are not) can only handle the (real) differences between clergy and laity, but are baffled by any vital, organic relationship between hierarchy and community. And yet, such is the real relationship: the ordained ministry acts *in* the community as the ministerial personification *of* the community — as the community's internal principle of identity and order. [33]

---

33. Cf. the analogous structure of the relationship between the infallibility of the Church and of the Pope as expressed in Vatican I (DS 3074): "[We declare] that the Roman Pontiff [...] enjoys *that* infallibility *which* the divine Redeemer willed his Church to be equipped with "([...] *Romanum Pontificem [...] ea infallibitate pollere, qua divinus Redemp-*

Sacraments and Ministry

By way of a third preliminary we must recall
that it is no longer felt to be an easy matter to
offer a definition of the sacrament of Order. In
this regard, modern theology is a far cry from the
heyday of textbook theology, which based its definition of the sacrament of Order almost entirely
on the liabilities it had inherited from the eucharistic disputes of the early Middle Ages and of
the sixteenth century. As a result, theology
strongly emphasized the power "to consecrate and
offer and administer the [Lord's] true body and
blood" (*[potestas] consecrandi et offerendi et
ministrandi verum corpus et sanguinem [Domini]* —
DS 1764; cf. 3316), much at the expense of other
offices of the ministry, such as the government
and development of the Church in spiritual matters
(DS 1311) and the continuation of the apostolic
mission and authority (DS 3450), both of them often considered secondary duties of the ordained
ministry. The New Testament, which always describes the apostolic office as authoritative service rendered to, and exercised in, the community,
requires that theology make an effort to restore a
unified, organic conception of the multitude of
tasks entrusted to the ordained ministry (not to
mention a fresh conception of the ministry entrusted to those without ordination). The basis
of this conception must be none other than the *diakonia* rendered to the Church — orderly service
aimed at ordering the life of the Church. The
Church herself, therefore, defines the sacrament of
Order; whatever the Church does to consecrate herself to the Father in the Spirit and by incorporation into Christ, she does through the ministry of
her ministers. Again it is clear that the sacrament of Order cannot be a separate, irreducible
entity of a wholly different nature, for it is
entirely defined by reference to the Church. [*34*]

---

tor Ecclesiam suam instructam esse voluit). Note that the
text does not say "the same ... as", or "a similar ... as",
but "that ... which", thus implying that there is only one
infallibility, not two separate infallibilities.

34. This does not mean in the least that it is a mis-

103

Church and Ordo

Before dealing with the conferral of the sacrament
of Order, it is useful, after the pattern set by
the dogmatic constitution of the Council of Trent
(DS 1763-1770), [*35*] first to make a few points
about the sacrament of Order as it actually functions in the Church (cf. the tenor of the first
two chapters, DS 1764-1765) [*36*].

take to put the ministry of the Eucharist at the heart of
the sacrament of Order. Quite the contrary. The traditional doctrine that apart from "power over Christ's mystical
body" (*potestas in corpus Christi mysticum*), the priest has
also "power over Christ's 'physical' [= real, true] body"
(*potestas in corpus Christi physicum*) is completely right,
no matter how clumsy and misleading the formula. We would
prefer to put it as follows. The service rendered to the
Church as the Body of Christ reaches its sacramental climax
in the ministry of the Eucharist — the worship of the Father in the fellowship of the Body of Christ. The point is
again to restore the "power of consecration," broken adrift
and isolated for polemical reasons, to its vital and original
context: the Body of Christ which is the Church. — For a
very full study of the sacrament of Order, cf. Bernard
Cooke, *Ministry to Word and Sacraments, History and Theology*,
Philadelphia, 1976.

    35. The constitution dates from the last year of the
Council, when, especially under the continual pressure of
St. Charles Borromeo, the Council was hurriedly brought to
an end. The document shows clear traces of this background:
it disposes of a number of errors of divers sorts and conditions (cf. the canons of DS 1771-1778), without sufficiently
distinguishing between essential doctrinal matters and ecclesiastical customs. This means, of course, that the constitution, theologically speaking, is not a strong composi-
tion, so that it must be handled with caution.

    36. This method would, it may be suggested, afford a
fresh approach to several other sacraments, too. The notion
of sacrament can very well be applied to the way in which
those who *have been* baptized (confirmed, married) and those
who *have been* ordained function in the world and the Church
respectively. This should be done with as much emphasis as

The *Ordo* — here understood as the body of the clergy — functions as a service rendered to the community, organically integrated into it and authoritatively bearing witness to its faith. This authoritative witness, however, is also directed *to* the community in the name of Christ. The witness takes shape in word and deed, in prophetic preaching and cultic, sacramental celebration, both of them essential to the inner life of the community. In this way, the very persons of the ministers concretize for the community its own faith and its own ecclesial nature, as they authoritatively appeal to the community to believe and as they authoritatively preside at its celebrations. This appeal and this presidency, exercized "with the identity of Christ" (*in persona Christi* — DS 3850), therefore, also confront the community, and in that sense are opposed to it. Still, this could never mean that teaching and worship would become the property of the *Ordo*, which would then subsequently have the task to let the community have some of the wealth entrusted to them. Rather, the community finds itself organically structured around the bearers of the sacrament of Order. [*37*]

A parallel jumps to the eye here. Just as the faithful acceptance of the *kerygma* gets crystallized and concretized around the faithful acceptance of dogma, so the Church crystallizes and takes concrete shape around the *Ordo*. But there is more than a parallelism here; the two struc-

---

is usually done with regard to the sacramental rites in which individuals *enter upon* their respective functions. This would also have another advantage. If we are to say that a sacrament gives grace, this approach would make us think, not only of the immediate recipient of the sacrament, but also of the world and the Church in which and for which he or she functions sacramentally.

37. This forms the basis of the relationship between *Ordo* and church order. The structures of the Church organically grow around the *Ordo*; when these structures are also legally laid down, a body of law, the church order, takes shape.

Grounded in Love

tures are interrelated. The *Ordo* is in a special
way the guardian and teacher of dogma, insofar as
it holds the magisterial office; the Church is the
living response to the *kerygma*. [*38*] Thus the *Ordo* and the dogmatic deposit entrusted to it are
not only the crystallization points, but also the
touchstones of the Christian community's loyalty
to the Church and its orthodoxy in the faith.
 In this dynamic structure two things should
be kept in mind. Firstly, just as dogma never replaces the *kerygma* and orthodoxy never becomes the
substitute for faith, so the *Ordo* never replaces
the Church. The eschatological *Ecclesia* can only
stay alive on her way to the eschaton (*in via*)
thanks to the fact that she bears within herself
the supporting service of the *Ordo* as a principle
of harmony and concretization, in exactly the same
way as the *kerygma* needs the service and the "rule"
(*regula*) of dogma if it is to be expressed and understood. But if *Ordo* and dogma were to yield to
the temptation to set themselves up as autonomous
rules of law, they would in that very moment get
ossified, for they would get detached from their
ministerial function, their service to the Church
and the *kerygma*, both of which remain the vital
atmosphere of *Ordo* and dogma, outside of which
they cannot stay alive. Dogma and *Ordo* are essentially provisional; [*39*] they may never be allowed

---

38. Cf. Antonio Javierre's discussion of *paradosis ka-
ta diadochen* ("Notes on the Traditional Teaching on Apostolic Succession," in: *Concilium* 34, pp. 16-27), esp. p. 22:
"The *diadoche* is an essential organ in the structures of the
Church, as well as a *criterion* of truth." In the same volume, Johannes Remmers reminds us that the time-honored concept of *paradosis* (tradition) is older than the concept of
succession ("Apostolic Succession: An Attribute of the Whole
Church," *Ibid.*, pp. 36-51; reference p. 42.
 39. And therefore sacramental. The application of the
text "Thou art a priest forever" to a newly ordained priest
is of dubious theological value, or rather, it can be applied to every Christian. The priest is ordained to Holy
Orders precisely for the pilgrim state of the Church. Cf.
for this again above, pp. 63-64, and p. 21, note 15.

to tie salvation down to themselves in an exclusive or absolute way. They are real only insofar as they function in a service capacity — insofar as they help the Church and its faith shape and concretize themselves in the provisional structures of the pilgrim state; and they can only do so by relying on the vital forces at work in the Church and the *kerygma*, and not by relying on their own ordering function.

Secondly, there has never been any *kerygma* without dogmatic expression, and in the same way the Church has never existed without *Ordo* (cf. DS 3850). It is important to make this point explicitly, since the above reflections might lead one to think that Church and *kerygma* brought forth *Ordo* and dogma only after some time. The *Ordo* is not an organ of authority which took its origin *from* a purely charismatic, pre-ordinal situation, which some would like to identify as the "true Church"; rather, *Ordo* exists *in* the Church as her very own principle of order, and it is in its turn kept from sclerosis and juridical fixation by the living Church, just as dogma exists *in* the *kerygma* as its own principle of orderly profession of faith, and is in its turn kept from dogmatism and integralism by the vital forces of the living, kerygmatic faith. The eschatological Church has always been identically the apostolic, well-ordered Church, just as the living faith has always had its "true words," its reliable dogmatic formulas. Were this not so, Church and *kerygma* would be disincarnate, purely metahistorical, gnostic (un)realities. [*40*]

---

40. The Church "is not an amorphous mass of loosely connected believers; it is a structured community with various services and offices. About 175 A.D. the notion of apostolic succession in the hierarchy begins to be developed systematically, to counteract the Gnostic notion that tradition involves the oral communication of secret and mysterious doctrines; but this new development is tied up with the apostolicity of doctrine. Legitimate succession in the hierarchy ensures and safeguards the apostolicity of Christian doctrine; it guarantees the authenticity of the tradition

Grounded in Love

Still, it remains important to emphasize that
every expression of the *kerygma* and every form of
church order, not excluding the New Testament writings and the apostolic church orders, are in and
of themselves provisional; they shape the Kingdom
and make it really present, but in an incomplete
fashion. Even Scripture and the apostolic church
orders remain based on the living realities of *kerygma* and Church, although it must be added at
once that, owing to the historical nature of eschatological salvation, they occupy a *prototypical*
place; in that sense it is rightly said that the
original Word of God and the basic pattern of the
Church of God are presented to us in the apostolic
writings and the apostolic church orders.

Scripture and the apostolic church orders, we
have said, exist and continue to exist only within
the vital atmosphere of the *kerygma* and the Church;
although prototypical, they are not simply absolute, as appears from the fact that they arose in
an organic interplay with the primitive community
called together by the *kerygma*. The same thing
can be demonstrated in a different way, too, namely, from the fact that they never simply proved
their own identity and authenticity, but were le-
gitimized by the Church in course of time. The
apostolic Scriptures are prototypically and canonically the Word of God *also* because the Church recognized herself in them. Now there is more than
mere historical coincidence in the fact that this
process of recognition — known as "canon formation" — took place roughly between 120 and 200 A.
D., that is to say, exactly in the period in which
the Church also became consciously aware of her
apostolicity as represented by her episcopal church
order. [*41*] Ever since this process of recogni-

being handed down. But the bearer of this tradition is the
whole Church, and the agreement of the whole community of
believers is the proof and the criterion of its authenticity" (Johannes Remmers, *op. cit.*, pp. 43-44).

41. The forceful statements of authors like Hegesippus
(Kirch 69-70), Irenaeus (Kirch 124-126; 136ff.), and Tertullian (Kirch 191-194) must, therefore, be taken seriously

108

tion the apostolic Scriptures have remained the
canon — the touchstone of the authenticity of all
further dogma (in the broad sense of: profession
and expression of faith); [42] in the same way
episcopacy has continued to be the canon and
touchstone of all further developments of church
order, that is to say, of all the further elabor-
ations of structures in which the eschatological
community takes visible shape. The Apostolic Tradition in the Church is only secure when it is in
agreement with canonical Scripture and apostolic
episcopacy, which are the prototypical, exemplary
forms of church belief and church order. Though
prototypes, however, they are not exclusive. E-
ven if the privileged position of canonical Scripture and apostolic episcopacy is fully credited, it
must be maintained that further developments of doctrine and church order (fruits of the Church's vitality and not of the regulating hierarchy as
such) also embody the Word of God and the Church
of God according as they have been recognized as authentic by the hierarchy in organic interplay with
the community at large. Were this not so, post-
scriptural doctrine and post-apostolic church order could never be enforced under pain of sin and
under promise of salvation.

without being absolutized. "Even if one wholly accepts the
threefold division of the Church's function into presbyters,
bishops, and deacons as a meaningful and practical development, one cannot treat such a juridical definition, which at
most is the practical realization of *but one* possibility, as
if it were a dogmatic necessity. The rich beginnings of a
Church order in the New Testament leave plenty of room for
other possibilities in practice." (H. Küng, "What is the Essence of Apostolic Succession?", in: *Concilium* 34, pp. 28-35,
quotation pp. 30-31) One might say that it is of the essence of the apostolic church order that *episcope* (oversight)
is exercized, whether by *monepiscopoi* (single bishops) or
otherwise. — This idea, by the way, might also apply to some
ancient writings that never made it into the canon of Scripture.

42. Cf. H. Küng, "'Early Catholicism' in the New Testament as a Problem in Controversial Theology," in: *The Living Church*, London, 1963, pp. 233-293.

In this structure as a whole the continuation of the *Ordo* remains related to the *diakonia* — the service rendered to the community. In other words, the *entire* structure, the community with the *Ordo* contained in it, reproduces itself through history in such a way that the Apostolic Succession is and remains defined entirely with reference to the Apostolic Tradition, of which it is the ministerial concretization.

At this point two difficulties present themselves. Are we not running a double risk by defining the Apostolic Succession entirely with reference to the Apostolic Tradition? On the one hand, are we not making the authority of the *Ordo* dependent upon the consensus of the community, so that the ministry becomes nothing but a body of officials delegated by the community? And on the other hand, do we not place the Apostolic Succession entirely outside the current of history by wholly referring it to the Church as such, rather than defining it in terms of the handing-on of the sacrament of Order?

No delegation

The sacrament of Order does not formally consist in the consent of the people (*consensus populi*). This is implied by the following canon of the Council of Trent (DS 1777; cf. 1768): "If someone maintains [...] that orders conferred by [bishops] without the consent or the call of the people or those in civil authority are null and void, [...]: he is excommunicated" (*S. q. d. [...] ordines ab ipsis [episcopis] collatos sine populi vel potestatis saecularis consensu aut vocatione irritos esse: A. S.*). Much clearer is the very careful formula of Pius VI in his condemnation of the Synod of Pistoia (DS 2602): "It is said that God gave the power to the Church so as to have it communicated to the shepherds, who are her servants for the salvation of souls; if this is understood to mean that the power to serve and guide the Church comes to the shepherds from the community of the faithful, it is heretical" (*Propositio, quae statuit, "potestatem a Deo datam Ecclesiae, ut communicaretur pastoribus, qui sunt eius ministri pro salute animarum"; sic intellecta, ut a communitate fidelium in pastores derivetur ecclesiastici ministerii ac regiminis potestas: — haeretica*). Finally, we have the following passage in Pius XII's encyclical on the liturgy, *Mediator Dei* DS 3850): "For there are people [...] who teach [43] that the only priesthood known to the New Testament is that which belongs to all those who have received the laver of Holy Baptism, [...] and that the hierarchical priesthood is only a subsequent, later development. Hence they maintain that the people enjoy true priestly power, and that the priest acts only on the basis of authority delegated to him by the community" (*Sunt enim [...], qui [...] doceant, in Novo Testamento sacerdotii nomine id solum venire, quod ad omnes spectet, qui sacri fontis lavacro expiati fuerint, [...] at exinde, deinceps tantum, hierarchicum consecutum esse sacerdotium. Quapropter populum autumant vera perfrui sacerdotali potestate, sacerdotem autem solummodo agere ex delegato a communitate munere*). Summing up, hierarchical power is not a derivative or delegated power, but an autonomous one. To use a phrase close to the definition of papal infallibility of Vatican I, it functions "in and of itself, not by the consent of the faithful" (*ex sese, non ex consensu fidelium* — cf. DS 3074: *ex sese, non autem ex consensu Ecclesiae*).

Two points should be made here. This kind of formula may never be allowed cajole us into reducing the whole matter into a black-and-white dilemma, or lead us to endorse the habits of thought that lead to this kind of dilemma. Secondly, the formula bears a marked resemblance to the formula "by reproduction, not by imitation of an example"

---

43. The full text specifies that these errors have already been condemned — *ad iam damnatos errores accedentes* — an allusion to Trent (DS 1777; cf. 1768); still *Mediator Dei* interprets the original decree rather more strictly than the text of Trent would seem to allow.

(*propagatione, non imitatione* — DS 1513) on original sin, and the formula already referred to,
"in and of itself, not by the consent of the
Church" (*ex sese, non autem ex consensu Ecclesiae*
— DS 3074 [*44*]) on the infallibility of papal
pronouncements.

In both cases just mentioned a highly polish-
ed juridical formula is used to make a statement
about an organic structure. In addition, both
formulas presuppose an individualistic view of human communication, whereas in fact this is personalistic and corporate. This leads to the conclusion that the distinctions made by the formulas
are not adequate, but inadequate; in fact, they
are inclusive, and even mutually inclusive.

Let us take original sin. Original sin is
also passed on by imitation of bad example; bad
example does condition others' behavior and conscious and unconscious choice. But the term "imitation" runs the risk of being misunderstood to
refer to purely extrinsic influence only; this
makes it necessary to stress that the essence of
our common human sinfulness is to be found at the
deepest possible level of the person: we are *born*
into a sinful human situation, which conditions
us down to the core (*propagatione* or *generatione*);
we do not just follow a bad example given on the
outside (*non imitatione*). Original sin, therefore affects the deepest strata of the person as
well as the community. If the term "imitation"
is understood to include these strata, too, it is
unobjectionable. [*45*]

Analogous remarks can be made with regard to

_____

44. In the spirit of the second Vatican Council we
would have to include a reference to the other bishops, to
do justice to collegiality; this was somehow also meant
by Vatican I, as appears from the proceedings. Cf. DS
3061, 3112-3117, 3310.

45. Still, it is sensible — on account of the historical Pelagian overtones of the term *imitatio* — to introduce a new term like "situation" or "being situated", as P.
Schoonenberg has done. Cf. his *Man and Sin*, London, 1965,
pp. 18ff.. Cf. also above, pp. 90-91, note 18.

papal infallibility, rendered by the formula that says that *ex cathedra* papal definitions are irreformable "in and of themselves, not by the consent of the Church" (*ex sese, non autem ex consensu Ecclesiae* — DS 3074). The consensus of the bishops and ultimately of the whole Church, to which the Pope, too, makes his contribution in an ordinary fashion, is much more than the sum of individual convictions; it is the moral consensus of a corporate body, which finds its unity concentrated and embodied in the person of the Pope. [46] The infallibility of papal pronouncements, therefore, does not exclude, but rather includes, the consensus of the bishops and the Church, just as the primacy does not detract from the authority of the bishops, but protects, safeguards and confirms it, which is precisely the specifically papal ministry. In an analogous way, too, the unity of each local Church is embodied in the person of the bishop, who, while being a member of the Church, is yet more than its representative and the witness to its faith; rather, he bears witness to and safeguards and confirms (and sometimes defends) the unity of his Church with the weight of his very person. [47] This is completely in accord-

---

46. Cf. DS 3310. This proves that collegiality does not exclude or diminish the primacy (as quite a few worried Ultramontanes tended to think at Vatican II), but actually requires and enhances it. In the voice of the Pope the moral consensus of the bishops must find its own confirmation and ultimate authority. — If we may apply this to a wholly different subject: If concelebration is a collegial act, there is no reason why the common consecration could not be *voiced* by only one (principal) celebrant; the latter does not exclude, but includes, the concelebrants. The factor "collegiality" is a new one in this discussion, so that DS 3928 (cf. above, p. 16, note 8) cannot be alleged as a statement of principle in this matter.

47. Here we may find the theological justification of the extraordinary ministry of the sacrament of Order exercised by the abbots mentioned above, pp. 81, 89-90. Not the authorization by means of a papal bull, but the situation — in this case, the unity of the monastic community and the

ance with the traditional view that the bishop
presides over his Church "with the identity of
Christ" (*in persona Christi*); the second Vatican
Council even says that he is "the vicar of
Christ" (*vicarius Christi*) in his Church. This
does not in the least imply that the bishop's
authority comes to him with absolutely no reference to his Church; the local Church, too, is the
Body of Christ, and if the bishop is the vicar of
Christ, he merely embodies, in his person, what is
also the deepest reality of the Church he presides
over. The bishop both embodies the local Church
and stands over against her. The latter feature is
especially prominent if it is remembered that the
bishop, in virtue of his membership in the college
of bishops, must also guarantee the local Church's
communion with the *Catholica*.

The most balanced expression of this structure as it applies to the primacy is found, as we
have pointed out several times already, in the
pronouncement of the first Vatican Council on papal infallibility (if for the moment we overlook
the fact that the role of the episcopal college is
implied rather than expressed): "We declare that
the Roman Pontiff speaking *ex cathedra* [...] enjoys that infallibility which the divine Redeemer
willed his Church to be equipped with; *for this
reason* such papal definitions are irreformable in
and out of themselves, and not by the Church's
consent" ([...] *definimus: Romanum Pontificem, cum
ex cathedra loquitur, [...] ea infallibilitate
pollere, qua divinus Redemptor Ecclesiam suam [..]
instructam esse voluit:* ideoque *eiusmodi Romani
Pontificis definitiones ex sese, non autem ex consensu Ecclesiae, irreformabiles esse* — DS 3073-3074.
With due changes, this also applies to the local Church.

We stated earlier that Apostolic Succession
must be entirely defined with reference to Apostolic Tradition. We can now add that this is so because it is by the ministry of the bishop that the

---

faithful in the region around the abbot as the focal point —
made this extraordinary ministry recognizable as an authentic service to the Church.

specific corporate unity of the local Church is organically shaped and ordered, and it is by the ministry of the pope surrounded by the college of bishops that the corporate unity of the whole Church is shaped and ordered. The Apostolic Tradition comes, so to speak, to a head in the Apostolic Succession; the latter is the organic embodiment of the former.

The idea of Apostolic Succession

So far we have only dealt with the sacrament of Order as it actually functions in the Church. The question about the nature of Apostolic Succession, however, has brought us to the point where we must examine the sacrament of Order as it is brought about — how do individuals enter upon their function as ministers of God's Church?
    Salvation in the Church is historical. The Church is Apostolic *Tradition*: the Church concretizes herself in the course of history after the patterns set by the canonical Scriptures and the apostolic, episcopal church orders. But the question is, is the *Ordo* in the Church continued as the Church is continued, or is it the only channel through which the sacrament of Order is handed on? In other words, is Apostolic Succession entirely defined in terms of Apostolic Tradition, or is it the instrument of its own continuation? [*48*]

---

48. The matter eventually boils down to the question whether episcopal consecration is necessary. "The older formula of this principle was: *'Quare soli Episcopi per Sacramentum Ordinis novos electos in corpus episcopale assumere possunt'* ['Why only bishops *can*, through the sacrament of Order, coopt new members into the body of bishops']; Vatican II substitutes for this a simple statement of fact: *'Episcoporum est per Sacramentum Ordinis novos electos in corpus episcopale assumere'* ['It *is* the bishops' task, through the sacrament of Order, to coopt newly elected members into the body of bishops']. (Bernard Dupuy, "Is There a Dogmatic Distinction between the Function of Priests and the Function of Bishops?", in: *Concilium* 34, pp. 74–86, quotation p. 83) — The same question may be put in a different way if we call

Before we go into the succession as it applies to the college of bishops, let us analyze
the notion of succession as it applies to the primacy. Traditionally it has always been said that
the Pope has no special powers of consecration
(*potestas ordinis*); in that regard, he is a bishop
just like other bishops. But it has always been
maintained that there is a qualitative difference
between the primatial office and the episcopal office, just as there is a qualitative difference
between the episcopal office and all the other offices in the Church. If, therefore, we can clarify the issue of papal succession, then — given the
parallel between the relationships Pope : Bishops
and bishops : church members — we may be better
able to clarify the issue of Apostolic Succession
as a whole.

According to generally accepted doctrine in
the Church the Pope is the successor of Peter (*Pe-
tro eiusque in hac cathedra successoribus* — DS
3071). This means, in concrete terms, that Pope
John Paul II is the successor of *Peter*, not the
successor of Pope John Paul I. Historically he
does indeed come after Pope John Paul I, but he
does not formally "succeed" him — a formal trans-

the papal bulls authorizing abbots to confer major orders to
mind again. In the monastic communities concerned the episcopal ministry was exercised by the abbot in an extraordinary way. If the privilege had not been discontinued (cf. DS
1146), a self-supporting local church in full communion with
Rome would have developed within the limits of abbatial jurisdiction; for if an extraordinary episcopal minister can
validly ordain priests, why could not one of those priests
— abbatial consecration not being a sacrament — in his
turn have proceeded to exercise the same ministry, once he
had become an abbot? In such an abbey, therefore, a kind of
extraordinary episcopate would have developed. Structural-
ly, the monastic community would have met the requirements
of the prototypical, episcopal church order; yet it would be
outside the mainstream of the historic Apostolic Succession.
This means that we can now put the question thus: Can an extraordinary ministry, if continuously recognized, become an
ordinary ministry in course of time?

fer of authority would have been needed for that.
How are we to understand the expression "succession
to the place of Peter" (*successio in locum Petri*)
then? The answer is: in terms of exemplarity.
Just as Peter prototypically functioned in the apostolic community and the primitive Church, so
John Paul II functions in the episcopal college
and in the Church now. The next question is: How
does the Pope get invested with this function?
The current answer is, as it has always been: by
accepting his election. The traditional analysis
of what happens in this election has yielded the
following theological interpretation. The cardinals, as the representatives of the Church of Rome
and of the Church Universal, elect the person, and
Christ invests this person with the apostolic authority. Still, it may be asked whether in this
analysis the activity of the living Christ is not
presented as too worldly, too "categorial", by being completely distinguished from, and then juxta-
posed to, the activity of the cardinals, to whom a
purely material election is attributed. The theory
gives the impression that the living Lord by a
separate intervention makes up for the fact that
the cardinals — or, for that matter, the pope-
elect himself — cannot make a Pope. It seems
better, therefore, to think of Christ's activity
as taking effect *in* the election of a Pope by the
Church, through the votes of the cardinals, and *in*
the pope-elect's acceptance of his election. For
it is the Church, the Body of Christ faithfully o-
bedient to her glorified Head, which finds herself
embodied in the person of the successor of Peter,
who receives his authority in the middle of the
Church, both "from" the Church and from Christ
"for" the Church. Thus he is not the delegate, but
the personification, the embodiment, the sacrament
of the corporate unity of the Church as Christ's
presence in this world.
    Now when a bishop enters upon his office as
the shepherd of a local Church, a double structure
takes effect. On the one hand he becomes the
bishop of this Church, and on the other hand he is

117

received into the college of bishops.

With regard to the first structure, his entering upon his ministry to the local Church, there is no handing down of authority by means of a transfer of powers on the part of the previous bishop. In other words, in this regard the same structure obtains on the local level and in the succession to the primacy: the bishop enters upon his office in virtue of his ministerial commitment to his Church. Writings like the *Didache* strongly stress the intimate connection between ministry and community: "Elect therefore (by raising hands? by imposition of hands?) for yourselves bishops and deacons worthy of the Lord" (15, 1). How about the situation during a *sede vacante* — the interregnum that follows a bishop's death or resignation and precedes the enthronement of a new bishop? The answer is that the only reality of episcopal rank in the local Church is then the empty see — the *cathedra* which is the focal point of the local Church.

But the local bishop is also a member of the college of bishops, into which he is received at his consecration. The unity of the local Church is an open unity; in the person of her bishop the local Church is in full communion with other local Churches in the persons of their bishops, and ultimately with the Church Universal in the person of the bishop of Rome. It is not surprising, therefore, that entering upon the episcopal office is also a collegial matter. Thus the fourth canon of the Council of Nicaea (325 A.D.) lays down: "It is most appropriate for a bishop to be made by all [the bishops] in the eparchy. If this should be difficult, either on account of an emergency or because of the length of the journey involved, at least three [bishops] should assemble for this matter, while the others should give their consent in writing. In each eparchy the confirmation of the procedure lies, by absolute right, with the metropolitan." [49]

---

49. As a result of this canon Athanasius was the first patriarch of Alexandria to be consecrated by episcopal lay-

The question is now: Is the consecration by
three (or more) bishops synonymous and identical
with Apostolic Succession, or is the former no
more (and no less!) than the concretization, laid
down by the church order, of the latter? In the
first case it would follow that the *Ordo* is the
only channel through which the sacrament of Order
is passed down; in the second, the rule would allow for exceptions, in the sense that the exceptions would lay bare the foundations on which the
canonical provisions are built.

It is a striking feature of the bishops'
lists, by which some ancient Sees authenticated
their claims to apostolicity (cf. Kirch 126, 191-
194), that the *point* of the *census* or list is the
apostolic character of the series. The point, in
other words, is not the chain of transfers of authority, but the fact that there is continuity
down to an apostle or an apostolic figure. The
consistent teaching of the Church has in fact been
that the bishops "succeed to the place of the
apostles" (*succedunt in locum Apostolorum* — cf.
DS 1768), which in light of the second Vatican
Council refers not only to the function of each
individual bishop in his Church, but also to the
function of the entire episcopate in the Church U-
niversal. By this emphasis on the "place" (*locus*)
— that is to say, the function — of the apostles
the full weight of the pronouncement is brought to
bear on the prototypical, exemplary nature of the
apostolic church order. Just as the apostles
functioned in the primitive communities, so the
bishops function in the Church now. The exemplary
nature of the relationship is the content of the
statement that there is Apostolic Succession in the
Church.

---

ing-on of hands; cf. above, pp. 82-83, esp. note 8. The
practice of consecration by three bishops was much older in
the West, as may be inferred, for instance, from the story
of the unlawful consecration of Novatian, who furnished
three rural Italian bishops with plenty of wine and availed
himself of their drunkenness to get himself consecrated. Abuse is a good witness to fixed custom! The date: 250 A.D..

This emphasis on the prototypical function of
the apostles leads to an emphasis on the ministerial, and in that sense charismatic, nature of episcopacy. For if indeed the function of the apostles provides the starting-point and the backbone
for the statement that there is Apostolic Succession in the Church, then the latter is not primarily viewed as the passing down of powers legally
established and isolated from the community, but
as the continuation of an organic structure, in
which the episcopal ministry is continuously defined with reference to the community. We have
already stated that it is precisely this ministry,
this *diakonia*, in the community which is the key
(in scholastic terms, the formal) element in the
sacrament of Order. Material, temporal succession
as such, the transmission of the authoritative
ministry, makes sense only if it is understood
that authority to *serve* is passed on. The concrete way of handing down this authority remains
based on the idea of ministry understood as service, and may never be allowed to detach itself
from it, to lead a separate, pipe-line existence.
The latter would amount to an unwarrantable tying-
down of the grace of the apostolic ministry to a
merely temporal, historical chain of events.
     Like everything in the Church, the continua-
tion of the ministerial structures has been regu-
lated by the church order. Yet it remains important to point out that this codification, however
right and understandable and serviceable in itself, can easily be misunderstood. The bishops in
the Church are the ministers of the community in an
organic interplay with it; but the church order,
with its specifically juridical terminology, unable
to express an organic structure in a simple formula, gives the impression that there is a black-and
-white relationship between the bishop and his
Church: either somebody is a bishop, or he (or she)
is not. In the same way the continuation of the
hierarchical structure of the Church is the result
of an organic interplay between the *Ordo* and the
community: even as the Church actualizes herself

Sacraments and Ministry

"through the ministry of the Church's ministers"
(*per ministerium ministrorum Ecclesiae*), so the
Apostolic Tradition is handed down "through the
ministry of Apostolic Succession"; but again, the
church order understandably simplifies this into
a complete separation of powers: bishops have
"power of consecration and jurisdiction", whereas
the laity do not.
 In normal circumstances this division of
tasks is completely acceptable and so the rule of
law in this matter is hardly noticed, except as a
habitual way to test people's basic loyalty to
the Church. [50] He who disregards the church order in this respect acts, it must be assumed, a-
gainst the Church, not because the church order is
the only source of salvation, but because it is
the concrete shape of the mind of the Church, so
that failure to abide by the church order would be
a sign of bad faith with regard to the Church. In
normal circumstances no member of the Church will
object to the continuation of the *Ordo* through the
ministry of the bearers of the sacrament of Order
themselves, for the transmission of the apostolic
office is not felt to be tyrannically tied down to
a canonically prescribed procedure; the historical,
temporal handing down of the ministry is kept alive
by the fact that it is the channel for the transmission of *service*, not caste privilege.
 If the channel is consciously and in bad faith
interrupted, this is an act of bad faith against
the Church and leads to disintegration of the community. [51] But let us suppose that in a *bona*

---

 50. Cf. what has been said with regard to the concept
of sacramental validity and the function of law, above, pp.
46-51, 84-87.
 51. And because the essential unity of the Lord's community is pre-eminently celebrated in the Eucharist, the basic argument of *Apostolicae Curae*, although very narrow, is
right: the Eucharist, the sacrament of Order and the Church
are essentially tied together. This is not to say that the
conclusion of *Apostolicae Curae* is also correct. The document takes for granted the theory that a defective link in
the chain of ordinations renders all subsequent ordinations

121

fide community the episcopal office is exercised
in accordance with apostolic church order, so that
it may be said that the Apostolic Succession in its
formal aspects is exercised in good faith; let us
further suppose that, on account of extraordinary
circumstances, in which the rule of law was experienced as irrelevant to the situation and thus
suspended, the origin of the ministry was not the
result of episcopal consecration — that is to
say, of temporal, material succession. Could such
a community still be said to have the sacrament of
Order, at least in the sense that its ministry
could be recognized as sacramental because it
meets the essential requirement? [52]

Some conclusions

Let us suggest a few tentative, hypothetical conclusions drawn from our arguments. Four come especially to mind.
1. The competence of the minister is not a
separate, "extrinsic" condition for the celebration of a sacrament. It is *the Church* that celebrates the sacraments *through the ministry of her
ministers*, whose church membership gets a special
direction and point by their ordination. To express the same in sacramental terms: the sacrament
of Order, like all the other post-baptismal sacraments, is an intensification and specification
of Baptism, and as such it is also a sacrament of
faith and of the Church (*sacramentum fidei, sacramentum Ecclesiae*). If Baptism is the Christian's
basic "ordination", then being received into the
Ordo means being "ordained up".
2. The *bona fide* extraordinary celebration

invalid, which is at least debatable; and its assumptions
about the nature of "sacrificing priesthood" are open to
discussion. With regard to the latter issue, cf. John Jay
Hughes, *Absolutely Null and Utterly Void*, pp. 284-293, and
his second volume, *Stewards of the Lord*.
52. Cf. N. Sykes, *Old Priest and New Presbyter*, pp.
239ff. for "succession in office." Cf. also W. Telfer's remarks, above, pp. 82-83, note 8.

of a sacrament does not change the sacrament; in extraordinary celebrations, therefore, the same sacraments are celebrated as in the ordinary ones. In both cases it is the Church that celebrates and actualizes her salvation, in faith. [53]

3. When a church in good faith celebrates its sacraments through the ministry of a body of ministers as specified by the church order, then — provided the church order meets the requirements of "oversight" (*episkope*) — not only the sacraments thus celebrated, but also the ministry itself is *recognizable* as sacramental, that is to say, as the sacrament of Order. To quote George Tavard once again, "If a given Protestant church does recognize its ministers as eucharistic hierarchs (even with a totally different vocabulary, with another form of designation or ordination, with another concept of succession and with another theological frame of reference), I see no reason why the Catholic church should not take note of this fact and recognize the sacramental dimension of which this community has the experience, thus acknowledging its ministry as the authentic ministry of the Eucharist, without asking historical questions about the forms in which this ministry was transmitted. In other words, I would suggest that we extend to all Christian churches the principle which we apply to ourselves: it is not apostolic succession which makes the church Catholic, but the catholicity of the church which guarantees apostolic succession." [54]

4. "The day will come, we hope, when, with the help of adequate guarantees of the traditional

---

53. A former teacher of mine called to my attention the possibility of describing the extraordinary celebration of a sacrament in terms of a sacrament whose sign is reduced or even defective on account of an emergency, as in the case of the sacraments of Penance and Anointing of the Sick being administered to an unconscious person, the Eucharist being celebrated by a priest without a community participating, &c.

54. George H. Tavard, "Does the Protestant Ministry Have Sacramental Significance?", *Continuum* 6(1968)260-269, quotation 267.

doctrine on the *mysterium fidei* ["mystery of faith"]
and all opposition to the apostolic succession
having ceased, the proper consistency of the eucharist among our Protestant brethren will be recognized — in virtue of the principle of *Ecclesia
supplet* ["the Church supplies"] or of "economy"
in Orthodox terminology, *even if the principle
would have to be extended to situations where it
has as yet never been applied.* For the Church,
mistress of the sacraments, can decide thus." [55]

---

55. M. Villain, "Can There Be Apostolic Succession
Outside the Chain of Imposition of Hands?", in: *Concilium*
34, pp. 87-104, quotation p. 104. — The principle "the
Church supplies [namely, what is lacking in the objective
order]", known among the Orientals as "economy", refers to
the presumption that God's grace, entrusted to the Church,
overrides the obstacles put up by human frailty in cases
where the church order is not, or cannot be, observed.

FIVE:

Intercommunion: A Note on Norms*

THERE ARE few questions in ecumenical theology
which have, over the past forty years, and especially since the Faith and Order Conference at
Lund in 1952, been more vigorously discussed than
"intercommunion" in its divers forms and grada-
tions. Perhaps this has been so because it is
eminently practical, not only in the sense that it
finally gives the theologian a chance to score a
point whose import can be appreciated by the faithful at large, but also in the (sometimes more un-
comfortable) sense that joint worship and joint
sacramental celebrations, once tried for size, are
liable actually to shape the sensibilities of the
divided church bodies in an ecumenical direction.
    For this reason among others it has been
pointed out that the problem of intercommunion is
an ecclesiological problem, and not primarily a
sacramental one. [1] Yet, for all the clarity of

---

* The literature on this subject has become so vast
that I will not attempt to discuss it or even pretend to be
familiar with all of it. Volume 34 of the *Concilium* series
is helpful. The *Journal of Ecumenical Studies* has kept a
careful record of what has happened, with good critical and
constructive essays, those by H. Küng (5[1968]576-578) and
Robert Quirin (7[1970]531-536) being among the older. *One
in Christ* has an entire issue devoted to the problem as it
looked twelve years ago, with a fine survey of the theological issues involved by Camillus Hay, followed by a docu-
mentary article (5[1969]355-378; 447-479). Instead of dealing with the existing literature the present chapter intends
to deal, in a more general fashion, with the *theological*
problems of intercommunion in the area where ecclesiology
and sacramental theology have a common agenda to deal with.
    1. Tavard has made this point with regard to my "To-

125

the distinction, it must also be said that there is a fundamental connection between the two. If it is true that the Church as such is the original sacrament (*Ursakrament*), and that sacraments are self-actualizations (*Selbstvollzüge*) of the Church, then it is obvious that the problem of sacramental intercommunion provides the theologian with a possibility to articulate his ecclesiological position in terms of such crucial events as are the sacraments. So far in this book, we tried to interpret the present church practice in sacramental matters by placing it against the background of the Church's basic dynamics, which, we argued, are likely to appear in a particularly lively way in those situations in which the church order is experienced as inadequate to meet the needs of the concrete situation. [2] In other words, we argued that sacramental borderline cases can be clarified by viewing them as ecclesial situations that "bypass" the church order (*praeter ordinem*). In this

---

wards an Ecumenical Understanding of the Sacraments," *Journal of Ecumenical Studies* 3(1966)57-112, which was the original version of chapters 2-4 of the present book. He writes: "[...] two questions [...] are often confused: recognition of the Protestant ministry as possibly a valid eucharistic priesthood, and intercommunion. Van Beeck links the two problems at the end of his article. This, in my opinion, is a mistake. Recognition of ministry is the acknowledgement that ministers of other churches are "priests" in the Catholic sense; it is primarily a sacramental problem. Intercommunion is participation by the members of one church in the eucharistic worship of another; it is primarily an ecclesiological problem." (I mislaid the reference to this quotation and am now unable to retrace it.)

2. We used the terms "antepredicative" and "postpredicative" (above, pp. 69, 73), and "emergency situation" (above, pp. 84ff.). The latter term has excellent credentials in the history of Protestant theology, too; the earliest Reformers felt isolated from the true Church and the Gospel, because the bishops (and the princes that protected them) were unwilling to help in what they considered a necessary reform. This "emergency situation" (*Notlage*) left them no choice but to proceed without episcopal authority.

chapter the process is reversed, and the question becomes: Can ecclesiastical borderline situations be clarified by viewing them as extraordinary sacramental situations?

There is another reason, far less methodological, why it is imperative to pay close attention to intercommunion, namely, that it is practiced. The Decree on Ecumenism of the second Vatican Council makes allowances for some forms of intercommunion, [3] and there is an inceasing body of official inter-church regulations regarding the various possibilities of open communion, whether mutual or one-sided, intercommunion, intercelebration, and full communion. But added to this, there is increasing evidence that in many places, and among Christians of many churches, including the Roman Catholic Church, sacramental intercommunion is being practiced without the authorization of the governing bodies of the respective churches to which these Christians belong. It sometimes, but not always, can be fairly described as "participation by members of one church in the eucharistic worship of another church"; the incidents, widely published at the time, at the International Eucharistic Congress at Medellín, Colombia, and during the General Assembly of the World Council of Churches at Uppsala, Sweden, both as long ago as 1968, could indeed be described in these terms. But they were only the first, rather spectacular manifestations of practices which have been inconspicuously gaining ground, and in which there is very often far less certainty about (or even interest in) the question as to which particular church or ecclesial community is the (principal) celebrating agent. Now it is the task of the

---

3. It must be said, with regret, that the *Directorium* issued after the Council interprets the general principles of *Unitatis Redintegratio* in a very restrictive way, so that the original inspiration is done some injustice to. From the rest of this chapter it will become clear that I think that there are forms of intercommunion which cannot be legislated for, since the concept of canon law does not enter into their definition.

theologian — if indeed not of every Christian —
to explore and try to understand the facts of
Christian life prior to judging them, and so we
must deal with the unofficial, untidy, though u-
sually pretty vital intercommunion events. If we
don't, our interest in sacramental law and order
is shallow; again, we must go to the root.

Communicatio in sacris

It cannot fairly be denied that, ecclesiologically
speaking, there is a difference between those sacramental celebrations in which the ecclesiastical
borderlines are crossed with the backing of the
church order on the one hand, and those which are
not so authorized on the other hand. Still, they
both have this in common that they are instances
of *communicatio in sacris* [4] between separately
organized denominational bodies. Now the situation of ecclesiastical separation is not a purely
political one; it is conditioned by *theological*
convictions about church order and confession of
faith. This is the reason why the churches have
traditionally felt, and still feel, strong reser-
vations with regard to intercommunion, whether
authorized or not. The prevailing assumption is
that church order and creed are the concrete shape
of salvation in the Church's pilgrim state (*in
via*), [5] which implies that non-observance must
be construed as failure in loyalty to the Christian community and its faith; at the very least,
also in cases of authorized intercommunion, there
is danger of scandal and some loss of faith.

In the pre-ecumenical era this assumption was
so firmly established that the utmost clarity was
possible in the matter of inter-church relationships. And it was only after the ban on intercommunion was very firmly established that the question could be raised to what extent there was room for

---

4. To avoid this cumbersome Latin phrase, *communicatio
in sacris* is henceforth simply referred to as "intercommunion", which is, therefore, used here in a broad sense.

5. Cf. above, pp. 63-64.

exceptions, to allow individuals to attend "heretical" or "schismatic" worship in particular cases. Thus, the Code of Canon Law laid down: "A passive, or purely physical, attendance, for reasons of public office or position of prominence, at funerals, weddings and similar occasions of non-Catholics, is permissible, if there is a serious reason to attend. In cases of doubt the bishop's approval is required, and there may be no risk of lapse from the faith and scandal" (*Tolerari potest praesentia passiva seu mere materialis, civilis officii vel honoris causa, ob gravem rationem ab Episcopo in casu dubii probandam, in acatholicorum funeribus, nuptiis similibusque sollemniis, dummodo perversionis et scandali periculum absit* — can. 1258 § 2). Further applications of the same principle included permission to pray privately or even publicly with non-Catholics, receiving necessary sacraments at the hands of schismatic or heretical ministers when in imminent danger of death, attending non-Catholic services for purposes of study, &c., always with the express provision that scandal and loss of faith must be excluded. To sum up, the situation was like this: intercommunion being forbidden, it was legitimate only in the second instance to ask the question how far one could go without jeopardizing one's own or other people's faith.

It is clear that this kind of ban on intercommunion could not be prolonged in the climate brought about by the ecumenical movement. Ecumenism, after all, envisages more than mere truce; it wants to go forward on the road to unity willed and promised by Christ. And the goal of all Christian endeavor being the full communion in the Lord, a new light was shed on intercommunion: what else are sacraments but the celebrations of Christ's unifying salvation, bringing men and women together to worship the Father in the same Spirit? Hence a new question arose. Does intercommunion not become a *duty*, which only in the second instance allows for the question as to how far, regrettably, we cannot go yet?

This situation was the context in which the churches began to draw up new regulations with regard to those forms of intercommunion which were felt to be truly ecumenical as well as compatible with doctrinal honesty and ecclesiastical coherence.

Intercommunion: a problem of norms

If doctrinal honesty and ecclesiastical coherence — both of them symbols of faith and unity — are involved in intercommunion, then it is obvious that there must arise a problem of norms. Doctrinal honesty and ecclesiastical coherence do indeed function as norms, canons, touchstones, [6] but the trouble with them is that they are essentially derivative. The fundamental realities are faith and *agape*; doctrine and coherence are the concrete shapes of the former, and as such, they are essentially provisional. They are norms, but not fixed norms; they tend to slide, as the gradual extension of legitimate intercommunion over the last ten or fifteen years has proved. Establishing the concrete, permissible forms of intercommunion, therefore, is a matter, not of principle, but of discretionary judgment. And here we are at the heart of the issue, once we have realized that it is the task of the appropriate officers in the Church to make those discretionary judgements, in the interest of having "all things done decently and in order" (1 Cor 14, 40).

The heart of the issue; we might as well have referred to the biggest problem and the source of most of the unrest with regard to intercommunion. The problem arises not only at the center, where the authoritative officers of the Church find themselves, but also among those members of the Church that move closer to the borderlines. The former realize that they have to come up with a judgment; they have to draw the line somewhere — that is to say, they cannot help creating some tension and the kind of insecurity that goes with

---

6. Cf. above, pp. 63-64, 104-110

it. The latter tend to feel that the existing
regulations (if, that is, they feel that there
should be any at all!) invariably fall short of
the real situation — they fail to do justice to
the ecumenical realities. It is the old problem of the margin tugging at the center all over
again; let us investigate what are the particular
difficulties of both.

The norms derived from creed and church order

All worship, including sacramental worship, [7]
is celebration of unity in the Holy Spirit, in
the presence of Jesus Christ in the Church. Now
the unity of the Church is essentially a unity in
the form of communion — in other words, a unity
in the form of church order, the shape which the
Church's eschatological unity is taking while the
Church is in the pilgrim state.

In ecclesiological terms, therefore, we can
speak of the communion of all Catholics under the
Pope, of the communion of the Latin Churches in
the patriarchate of Rome, of the different communions of Oriental Churches, Orthodox and even Uniate, of the Anglican Communion, and so forth.
This kind of communion, however, will often take
the shape of "intercommunion" of larger units.

----

7. The traditional distinction between joint prayer
and reading of the Word on the one hand, and joint celebrations of sacraments on the other hand, though by no means
unreal, must not be exaggerated. Prayer and Bible services
are all too often permitted because "nothing happens" in
them — as if prayer and the Word were not in some sense
sacramental. On the other hand there is a tendency to view
joint celebrations of sacraments as acts of the most perfect
communio, which, therefore, will have to be postponed till
the day when official mutual recognition will be a fact. Is
this not to forget that communion in the pilgrim state will
never be perfect, and that it is *also* in the nature of a
sacrament to be a *pledge* of salvation? It seems not wholly
sound to view the sacraments as so eschatological as practically to deny that they are part of the Church's pilgrim
state. Cf. also above, pp. 60ff..

Thus the communion between Rome and the Uniate O-
riental Churches has many features in common with
such intercommunion patterns as prevail, say, between Anglicans and Old Catholics, and between
Anglicans and the Church of South India. The
characteristic feature of intercommunion is that
churches (or groups of churches) recognize each
other as churches through an explicit recognition
of each other's hierarchies and creeds, and through
agreements on canonical procedures involving both
partner churches, while at the same time allowing
for more or less far-reaching differences at the
level of church order, and of doctrinal, moral and
devotional sensibility. [8] As long as all churches are on the way to the eschaton, full communion
will always bear some of the characteristics of
intercommunion, witness the differences in out-
look, orientation and interests among the Latin-
rite churches throughout the world. In this provisional situation, episcopacy and ultimately the
primacy act as ministries to the unity of the
Church in the pilgrim state. This ministry, therefore, is sacramental: communion at the level of
the hierarchy is the real, though provisional,
presence of the eschatological communion.

At the second Vatican Council it was often
clearly stated that unity is not the same as uni-
formity. This amounts to saying that the one
Church can consist of larger units, each comprising a number of local churches. These units
would have the fundamental doctrines and church
structures in common, but also keep and develop
their own distinctive types of spirituality, liturgy, theological sensibility and church order,
mutually recognized and respected.

---

8. The Latin church has, since Trent, had great difficulty in giving this variety a palpable shape, witness
the long-standing struggle over the Code of Canon Law for
the Uniate Oriental Churches, and the hesitations of episcopal conferences to go about the shaping of their churches in a creative fashion. — Cf. also the beautiful article
by Edward P. Echlin, "The Uniate Model and Anglican Ministry," *New Blackfriars* 52(1971)386-396.

In light of the possibility, and even desira-
bility, of such a collegial, or synodal-federative,
conception of church unity, it is possible to take
a fresh look at the state of division in which the
Christian churches find themselves. Church communion, in this new perspective, becomes an active
process of communication; the canonical structures
of ecclesiastical communion are no more (and no
less) than the provisional framework for this process. This brings out the paradox of pluriformity — a pluriformity which is not a sign of bad
faith, as dissidence within the same church order
is, but rather a necessary and attractive feature
of the Church's pilgrim state. Mutual recognition,
it must be remembered, is a matter of canon law,
and hence it is not self-authenticating; we begin
to appreciate it, however, once we realize that it
is the framework in which *communio, koinonia, so-
bornost* — in other words, inter-church appreciation *through charity* of each other's faith and
activity is realized, provisionally and in faithful reliance on the Lord, "until he comes."

In light of the churches' ecumenical efforts,
made in obedience of faith, to communicate with
each other, the present state on division may very
well be described in terms of incapability (rather
than refusal) to recognize the faith and the Church
of Christ in each other's creeds and church orders. [9] But this in turn, so it would appear,
leads to some important questions regarding church
unity and sacramental intercommunion.

The first question is the following. What is
the intrinsic cogency of ecclesiastical norms for
intercommunion, given that these norms are essentially provisional, sliding and hence, ambivalent?
This felt ambivalence is further enhanced by the
inability-component involved in all intercommu-
nion-relationships, in that the norms lay down
what Christians of different churches can "already"
do, and what they can "not yet" do in the way of

---

9. Cf. John Meyendorff, "The Significance of the Reformation in the History of Christendom," *The Ecumenical
Review* 16(1964)164-179, esp. 178.

intercommunion. Doctrinal honesty and ecclesiastical coherence are noble causes indeed, but they
cannot prevent the regulations from looking a bit
unconvincing owing to this restrictive quality,
which moreover carries an element of arbitrariness
in it. And this restrictiveness is all the more
sharply felt according as Christians are more
aware that existing doctrine and church order represent the past rather than the future, the viewpoint of ecclesiastical order rather than the
challenge of ongoing revelation. The norms seem
removed from the struggle for truth that is going
on in the borderline areas between the churches
and the world.

The problem is not just one of restrictiveness, however; current regulations regarding intercommunion also evoke a sense of futility. If
church coherence and doctrinal honesty are essentially sliding, because they are derivative and
provisional; and if, moreover, their present importance is strongly contingent upon the shifting
fortunes of official ecclesiastical inability to
communicate with other churches' creeds and
church orders; and above all, if total congruence
in doctrinal climate and canonical order is not
only impossible but even undesirable: what, then,
is the "big deal" in having (or, for that matter,
not having) intercommunion? In other words, to
what extent is intercommunion, or even communion,
relevant to the Gospel and to life, and why?

This sentiment, already so widespread, must
be taken extremely seriously, for it touches on
the *problem of meaning*, both of church union and
of church division. Ecclesiastical exultation
about forms of intercommunion already achieved has
lately come to have a more and more unreal ring in
the ears of many Christians, as has the expression
of ecclesiastical regrets and hopes with regard to
the long road to unity yet to go. It must be admitted that there is probably a fair amount of
anti-doctrinal and anti-canonical animus in this;
still, the presence of the "third man" [10] in the

---

10. Cf. above, p. 33 and note 31.

churches is too obvious a phenomenon to be lightly dismissed. Discussing the norms of intercommunion leads to an impasse; we must move on to the problem of meaning if the norms are to make any sense at all.

Sign and cause: a dead end

The impasse of the discussion about the norms for intercommunion is, perhaps, best illustrated by the way in which the equal status of the sign-character and the cause-character of the sacraments is alleged to solve the problem. To those who want to jump the gun and go ahead with intercommunion, theologians and most church authorities say: "To say that the Eucharist is both sign and cause of unity does not entail that, in the absence of the unity to be signified, one may use it as a cause that may bring unity about. For signification and causality, in sacramental theology, are not two distinct qualities of a sacrament. Rather, the sign is the cause, effecting what it signifies. It does not antedate its effect (cause has no chronological content here); but it expresses its effect, which it inseparably manifests, in the two senses of realizing and showing. Sign and cause must be taken, to use scholastic language, *in sensu composito* ["as two elements of one reality"], not *in sensu diviso* ["as two mutually separable elements"]." [*11*] This reasoning, which not only has excellent speculative credentials, but also has the weight of Roman Catholic and Orthodox attitudes behind itself, is based on the following recognition: "[...] in our theology which recognizes a close bond between Eucharist and Church, there is *not much room* for intercommunion. How could there be eucharistic communion between separated ecclesiastical communions, while these two communions — the eucharistic and the ecclesiastical — are dependent on each other? [*12*]

11. G. Tavard, in the article quoted above, p. 125, note 1.
12. Jérôme Hamer, "Stages on the Road to Unity — The Problem of Intercommunion," *One in Christ* 4(1968)235-249,

The question presents itself, however, whether this appeal to the equal status of the sign-aspect and the cause-aspect in sacraments is really helpful in solving the impasse. The proposition is indeed beautifully balanced, so it might seem at first blush, but on closer inspection it becomes clear that, for the purpose of the debate on intercommunion, "sign" and "cause" are really played off *against* each other. The proponents of the official policy of very limited intercommunion will remind those who want greater freedom that a sacrament is not only a cause, *but* also a sign of unity, so that in effect the appeal to causality is kept in check by the appeal to signification. On the other hand, those who want to use intercommunion as a means to further the quest for unity will remind ecclesiastics that the sacrament is not only a sign, *but* also a cause, thus trying to break the limits set by signification by means of an appeal to causality.

If the debate continues to be carried on in these terms it will remain fruitless. This is so because the terms of the debate are faulty; as happens so often, conservatives and liberals agree on the terms of the debate, and differ merely on the conclusions. "Sign" in this debate is taken in far too noetic a sense; "cause" is understood in far to extrinsic, mechanical a sense; modern sacramental theology has long abandoned these unfortunate associations and taken "symbol" for its basic category — "sign" and "cause" must be understood in an anthropological context.

The two positions, however, have another assumption in common as well. They give the impression of thinking that church unity is, if not exclusively, then at least decisively, a matter of

---

quotation 242. Notice the expression "not much room"; when Hamer read this article as a speech at Berkeley on January 24, 1968, he said — according to Tavard — that "[...] there is *no room* for intercommunion." The version that appeared in *America* on June 1, 1968 (734-737) has: "[...] there is *no room* for intercommunion *as a common and normal practice*." (Italics in all quotations mine.)

communion or intercommunion. It turns out that
both conservatives and liberals in this case agree
with the classical definitions of Church unity and
sacramental communion in terms of each other; but
must we not ask the question: Is this not a closed
circuit view of the realities of Church and sacrament? True, there are strong differences between
the two. The advocates of the official policy
solve the problem by making signification and causality coincide in such a way that the *existing* u-
nity of the Church is signified, and then also enhanced by the efficaciousness of the sacrament.
The advocates of freer intercommunion solve the
problem by seeking a unity that *does not yet exist*
through the efficacious causality of the sacramental celebration; the unity that is already given
in Baptism is signified and expanded by the sacrament, and for one fleeting moment, the One True
Church appears in the sacramental sign — a sign,
which they hope will be cause for further unity.

We venture to suggest that both conceptions
represent a closed system — a closed system of a-
wareness, that is. The common viewpoint is an ecclesiological one: Church unity is conceived in
terms of sacramental celebration of communion, and
sacramental communion is conceived in terms of
Church unity. But this leaves two deeper, soteri-
ological questions unanswered. They are: 1. What
is Church unity *about?* [13] And: 2. What is a
sacrament *about?* Let us try to develop an answer
to the first question in terms of the second.

Sacraments and concern: a way out

All symbols, sacraments not excepted, have this in

---

13. In asking this question I am implying that Church
unity and authorized intercommunion based on ecclesiastical
and hierarchical agreement are not self-authenticating. They
must basically be about something else, otherwise they have
a tendency to degenerate into ecclesiastical self-gratification. Cf. again what was explained above, pp. 63ff.. The
question that we must keep asking in this area is: What values are served by unity, or by intercommunion?

common: they create an environment in which people
can communicate. This environment is created by a
symbolic re-enactment of an event, whether historical or "mythical," and it is in the re-enactment
that the memory, the meaning, and the abiding presence of the past event literally come to life in
the present — that is to say, they are applied
to, and revivified in terms of, present concerns.
The reverse also takes place: present concerns are
interpreted and experienced in a new perspective
in the light of the past event, whose re-enactment
suffuses the present concern with direction and
meaning. In the symbolic celebration order and
perspective, faith and hope are wrested from present chaos, in the name of the past and with an eye
to the future. For a few precious and precarious
moments people who struggle to make sense out of
confusion and communion out of alienation catch a
glimpse of the promised land by invoking a past
experience in whose light the confusion of the
present is experienced as the womb of a new birth.

A symbolic celebration is not a repetition of
a past event nor a wistful re-enactment of a past
communion that has forever become a thing of the
past; [14] rather, it consists in having the reality of the past event and the realization of the
past communion brought to bear on the concerns and
struggles of the present. The past event that is
celebrated is at once greater and smaller than the
present concerns. It is greater insofar as it has
the capacity to "absorb" the present concerns and
thus to suffuse them with its meaning and a sense
of direction; it is smaller insofar as it is experienced as somehow incomplete, and in need of re-
enactment in terms of new concerns that arise.

Now the motor force of this dynamic lies in
the concerns of the present. It is in the face of
present confusion that people who believe that the
seed of meaning is hidden in this madness reach

----

14. In the terminology of sixteenth-century Catholic
eucharistic theology: a symbolic celebration is neither a
repetition (*repetitio eiusdem*) nor a purely mental recalling
(*nuda commemoratio*) of a past event.

out for what they believe is the ultimate meaning. Apart from this struggle with present concerns, any celebration will become an empty gesture of what Bonhoeffer called "Religion", an abdication of responsibility, and an exercise in self-gratification and self-appeasement. Cut loose from a lived awareness of distress — in traditional terms: cut loose from the felt need for redemption — symbolic celebrations tend to move in the direction of blasphemous magic practiced in a closed circle.

It is necessary to be realistic here. Present concerns are usually somewhat confused; that is to say, they are unthematized, unchanneled, and in that sense unredeemed, unarticulated and unintegrated. They represent the messiness of ordinary life, the vital but somewhat disconcerting (and sometimes even threatening) grey area between light and darkness, where people struggle for identity, communication and direction. But this area, which Paul refers to as the *biotika*, the realities of life (1 Cor 6, 3) [15] is precisely the stuff of regeneration. The redemption and the harmony that come out of the struggle for identity and communication and direction are sealed by the symbolic celebration, presided over by the living Lord, who lived our life, died out death and is the hope of the glory to come. Every celebrating community has to view itself essentially as a community that struggles for an ongoing articulation and integration of the realities of life, if it is to remain true to life as well as true to its own deepest inspiration.

If we apply this brief sketch to the problem of sacramental celebrations and intercommunion, we can draw the following conclusions.

---

15. The themes of 1 Corinthians are highly pertinent to the content of this chapter, especially the idea that salvation has to be worked out in *agape*, the theme of concern for others in the business of ordinary life, and the idea that sacramental initiation does not provide a guarantee of salvation, unless it is referred to practical life: 1 Cor 10, 1-13; 11, 23-24.

The first conclusion deals with the celebration of the sacraments — and especially of the Eucharist — *within* a certain ecclesiastical community. The existing unity of the Church as such provides insufficient grounds for the celebration of the Eucharist; in and of itself, it is no more than a closed system. The community that really celebrates the Eucharist is the community in its pilgrim state (*in via*) — that is to say, the community that struggles for further unity in Christ by letting Christ's redemption be brought to bear on its worldly concerns. This amounts to saying that the Eucharist is celebrated precisely by the Church in so far as she *is* a borderline situation, in the world but not yet quite redeemed from the powers of this world, seeking assurance in Christ while still halfheartedly clinging to the transitory assurances of the world, reconciled to God in Christ but as yet also alienated from God by the power of sin. As soon as the celebration of the Eucharist were to become no more than a premium on being a Christian community in good standing, or, in different words, as soon as the dynamic interplay between the Christian life and participation in the Eucharist were to flag, the Church would harden in her pilgrim state, and the Eucharist would turn into the Egyptian fleshpots instead of remaining a *viaticum*, a wayfarers' dole in anticipation of the messianic banquet. Both the Church and the Eucharist would, in other words, lose their meaning.

If, however, the dynamism between the Christian life and the Eucharist is kept alive by an awareness of concerns to be incorporated into the body of Christ, then the celebration of the Eucharist within the bounds of each Church is indeed an "authentic means toward unity," as Jérôme Hamer has rightly pointed out; [*16*] in such a case, the unity celebrated would not be any closed ecclesiastical circle, but a unity that seeks to be open to the world. It is precisely for this reason, namely, that the unity of the Church should be a

_____
16. *Op. cit., 246.

unity that is instructed by, and embraces, the
cares and concerns of the world, that the unity of
ecclesiastical order and the unanimous endorsement of the propositions of the creeds and the
confessions are not the most fundamental norms for
the common celebration of the Eucharist. [17]
    A second conclusion is the following. Since
vital concerns are more liable to occur on the
borderline between Church and World than at the
center of the Church (where the tendency to stabi-
lize faith by means of doctrine and *agape* by means
of church order is the strongest), they are also
more liable to occur in the borderline areas between the separated churches, where the *biotika* (1
Cor 6, 3f.) — the human predicament with all its
"crudities, doubts, and confusions" [18] — , in
short, where "life and work" have Christians from
different churches, as well as non-Christians, u-
nited in a common struggle for meaning. In view
of what has been already said it would seem legitimate to conclude that there is room for common
sacramental celebration in such cases, since unity
in creed and church order is not the ultimate norm
for sacramental celebration. It is important to
be clear here. Such groups of Christians do not
have a *right*, let alone a *duty*, to have joint sacramental celebrations, nor do they have to do so
because such celebrations would be an excellent
means to foster Christian unity (or to shake conventional Christians out of their complacency!).
Rather, we would like to suggest, such celebrations are likely to arise because, given their
common faith in Jesus Christ, Christians like that
may feel they cannot help celebrating the sacraments together.

---

17. A prominent American liturgist with a reputation
of long standing once remarked, I am told, that the average
suburban Sunday congregation "has no right to celebrate the
Eucharist." In the context of this chapter the same hyper-
bole could be expressed, oddly enough, by maintaining almost
the opposite: the *only* thing complacent Sunday congregations
have is the canonical *right* to celebrate the Eucharist.
    18. Dylan Thomas, *Collected Poems*, London, 1952, p. vi.

141

It is obvious that in so doing these Christians take a risk. Their action cannot possibly be guaranteed by their churches as such, and consequently all kinds of questions arise regarding scandal, loss of faith, validity and invalidity. But these doubts and insecurities are the normal concomitants of actions that take place outside the letter of the law (*praeter ius*) [19], and besides, it is good to recall a few points. First, what from the point of view of ecclesiastical order and orthodoxy (which is a valid but essentially derivative point of view) may seem to represent loss of faith and scandal, may very well prove to be the beginning of considerable gain in the kind of Christian unity that would do justice to the Gospel as well as to the modern world, and whose church order would be more flexible and whose creed would sound more lifelike. Second, there is — oddly enough — a good deal of *im*patience involved in the overemphasis on the need "to wait in patience until the sense of the church comes into the open," and meanwhile to brand all forms of unauthorized intercommunion in experimental ecumenical situations as "wild-cat intercommunion" (G. Tavard). And finally, if validity is the Church's warrant for the effectiveness of a sacrament, this does not entail, not even purely logically speaking, that invalidity is the Church's warrant for a sacrament's *in*effectiveness. [20] This realization should help people override some of their overconcern with the issue of validity and invalidity in informal intercommunion.

The situation of the minister
as a reflection of the Church's predicament

The present crisis in the churches, of which the ecumenical movement, with all its promises and impasses, is but one element, affects the middle and lower echelons, that is to say, ministers, priests

12. Cf. above, pp. 88-100.
13. This point has been very well made by John Coventry: "Valid," *Faith and Unity* 12(1968)91-93.

and religious, and generally all people involved in the Church at the local level, most of all. [*21*] Hence, it is not surprising that the "ordinary clergy" and those immediately surrounding them find themselves in the midst of a conflict of roles and loyalties the moment the issue of inter-communion comes up. It would seem worth while, therefore, to articulate the ecclesiological pro-blem [*22*] of intercommunion in terms of the situa-tion which the minister finds himself in, and more particularly, the minister in good standing, [*23*] and even more particularly, the minister who is occu-pied full-time in the most conventional, least charismatic, and most run-o'-the-mill ecclesias-tical framework: the parish.

Catholic theology has, over the past decades, come to redefine the ministry. Ministry is now defined in terms of the Church as a whole, and on-ly *within* that setting is it defined in terms of the sacramental celebration of the Eucharist and the authoritative ministry of the Word. This has important consequences. First of all, it has led to a more comprehensive, pastoral conception of the ministry: the minister is the appointed person to provide guidance to the Christian community as such, and within that context he is, therefore,

---

21. Observation made by the Dutch sociologist H. P. M. Goddijn, quoted in my "The Practice of Obedience and Author-ity in the Dutch Church," in: J. Dalrymple and others, *Au-thority in a Changing Church*, London, 1968, pp. 138-161; re-ference p. 159.

22. In other words, the doctrinal aspect and the ques-tion of the validity of orders, discussed elsewhere in this book, are not brought into the picture here.

23. It is well-known that the "underground" church frequently uses the services of priests, married or unmar-ried, who have been officially suspended from the active ministry. I think it is legitimate to ask the question as to what value must be attributed to ecclesiastical suspen-sion. Still, I think it is also legitimate to wonder to what extent this practice in the underground church is pre-dicated on the dubious assumption that the power of conse-cration is, and remains, the ordained priest's own property.

the appointed minister of the Word and the sacraments. In other words, his function exceeds the
role of the appointed celebrating and authoritatively preaching official; he is, comprehensive-
ly, the appointed minister and the sacramental exponent of the believing community as such. Secondly, it would be too narrow a conception of the
ministry to look upon it exclusively as a service
to the community of believers. The entire community of believers and each believer individually
form a community of service to the world, and any
service undertaken by the ordained ministry must
enhance this service to the world, and direct itself to the world in some fashion. The *Ordo* finds
its basis in the common priesthood, and if the
latter is a service to the world, the former cannot be reduced to an exclusive service to the
Church. [24] By being ordained, clergy do not
give up their vocation as Christians!
But it is precisely at this point that the

---

24. For the expression "ordained up," cf. above, p.
122. Cf. also an important article by Robert McAfee Brown:
"New Perspectives on the Problem of Ministry and Order,"
Journal of Ecumenical Studies 4(1967)497-484. — The present
chapter views the priest primarily as the ordained exponent
of the community; this is not in derogation of his position
as Christ's authoritative representative *over against* the
community (above, p. 105). — Finally, let me conclude this
note with a parting shot and a leading question. When sur-
veying the increasing series of committee-reports coming out
of the doctrinal conversations between the major churches of
late, one is struck by the far-reaching consensus on almost
every issue discussed. The one question that so far has
proved the worst obstacle to unity is the churches' understanding of the ministry. I grant that this betrays a deeper ecclesiological problem; still I find myself asking the
question, Are the churches being kept apart by the clergy's
jealous defense of its own self-image? Religious profes-
sionals have their own besetting sins, and we must ask ourselves if we are not replicating the situation Jesus found
himself in: Pharisees, Sadducees, priests and Levites, etc.;
to the extent that this is so we'd better remember that the
Lord refused to identify with any of them.

conflict begins to arise. The Eucharist has always
— emphatically in the Roman Catholic and Orthodox
traditions, but also with varying degrees of emphasis in the churches of the Reformation — been
called the center of the Church, her highest mani-
festation and her constitutive force: it is in the
Eucharistic Body of Christ that the Mystical Body
of Christ finds its unity and identity. Still, in
spite of the venerable tradition behind this statement, a distinction is in order. When we say that
the Eucharist is the center of the Church, attention must be paid to the fact that this is a sacramental statement. Now sacramental reality is
not all of reality, except in a symbolic sense;
but then again, there is more to life than symbol-
ization. Now some will say that everything — not
just the formal sacraments, but everything — the
Church or any of her members do is sacramental;
but then we must remember that the Eucharist is a
sacramental celebration; and again, there is more
to life than celebrating. The life and work of
Christians at large is as integral to the Church
as her symbolic, sacramental celebrations. The
former without the latter would lead to the disappearance of the Church as a community of worship; the latter without the former would lead to
the disappearance of the Church as a community of
effective witness and service.
    Now it so happens that the gift of the Spirit
does not always coincide with celebrations; where-
ever concerned Christians put themselves on the
line with an appeal to the life, death and resurrection of Jesus Christ, "Church" takes place.
There was a relationship between the Last Supper
and the actual life and death of the historical
Jesus; an analogous relationship must be reflected
today in the relationship between the Eucharist
and the living surrender of concerned Christians
moved by the Spirit. The unity of the Church is
not only enacted and celebrated in sacramental
fashion, but also built up and actualized in "real
life," no matter how unclear, and even how unacceptable, the risks undertaken and the concerns

defended may seem to other Christians, especially
when compared with the worshipful, quiet, orderly
and familiar dignity of the sacramental celebration.
    And there's the rub. The Eucharist is cele-
brated within the confines of each church, and so
the minister, insofar as his function is essentially determined by his eucharistic ministry,
finds himself tied down to a church whose boundaries he feels he can hardly cross. In the mean
time the Church as a missionary happening, actualized by the struggle of Christians whose concerns
take a rather more centrifugal direction, invariably occurs in areas where denominational borderlines are increasingly mellowed, and even sometimes wiped out, by common concerns. When faced
with this sort of experience, the clergy in their
capacity as pastors who owe guidance to the Church
at large often find themselves at loggerheads
with themselves in their capacity as eucharistic
ministers. Thus, quite apart from any doctrinal
questions regarding the nature of the eucharistic
function of the ministry — ranging all the way
from the concept of "sacrificing priesthood" to
"mere presidency" — , the very fact that the
ministry in the Christian churches is an ordained
ministry becomes an ecumenical problem.
    In virtue of his ordination, it is true, the
minister is called to act as a principle of order
and coherence in the community, in the area of
doctrine as well as church order. He must keep
the community together. But we must keep in mind
that "order" in the Church is not something entirely self-authenticating; it is a function of
agape, which binds the community together in Jesus Christ, that is to say, in a comprehensive
concern for its own members as well as for the
world. The loyalty which the ordained minister
owes to the Church as such may never be so nar-
rowly interpreted as to exclude any *ministerial*
participation in the concerns of those members of
the community who move in the borderline areas
between the churches and the world. In other

146

words, granted that the minister needs to use a lot of sound discretionary judgment in order not to scandalize the members of the community, neither the minister's concern for the Church as such, nor his declared loyalty to his own church's creeds and church order make it *a priori* impossible or unwarrantable for him in particular cases to draw the sacramental consequences from certain interdenominational pastoral situations. If and when he or she does this, he or she interprets his or her sacramental function in the light, not of church order, but of the dynamics of concern, and he or she proceeds to celebrate, or con-celebrate, the Eucharist on the crossroads between church and church, and between Church and World.

It is important to note at this point that in doing so the minister is not employing the celebration of the Eucharist as a "means" to further the unity of the churches, nor does he or she go against the church order in the sense of committing a gesture of wilful disregard or defiance against the shape of the Church in her pilgrim state. The celebration, rather, would be based on the recognition that, if sacraments celebrated *within* a particular church are to be celebrated with a view to concerns, real concerns shared by Christians may lead to celebrations of sacraments straddling the fences between the churches. Now to postulate, in the face of real, existing concerns, that those who are part of the Church's *Ordo* can never bypass the church order (or, as we have put it, "act *praeter ordinem*") would be as shortsighted as to demand that they *must* do so in the interest of furthering church unity.

To sum up, we must recognize that a minister meets with situations in which he or she is torn between loyalty to the established community of faith and loyalty to the meeting-grounds, as yet unexplored, between the churches and the world. This recognition might prove one of the most important ways for the churches to recover that precarious balance between centripetal and missionary dynamics, which is the essence of *agape*: love of the brothers and sisters in Christ and a deep concern with the world that is to be saved. In that sense, too, the responsible freedom with which the churches would apply their church orders may show to the world and to the countless Christians for whom the church order has become quite empty that ecumenism is not just an exercise limited to the level of Faith and Order, but also a practice firmly rooted in Life and Work, and that ultimately the attitudes of faith, hope and unity expressed and celebrated by the churches are truly "grounded in love" (Eph 3, 17).

Index of Proper Names

ABOUT THE AUTHOR

Born in the Netherlands in 1930, Frans Jozef van Beeck joined the Jesuit order in 1948 and was ordained to the priesthood in 1963. He pursued graduate studies in his native country, in philosophy (1951 - 4), English and Italian literatures (1954-60; Ph.D. 1961), and theology (1960 - 4; S.T.L. 1964). He has taught sacramental and systematic theology at Boston College since 1968. Besides a baker's dozen articles on literary and theological subjects in a variety of periodicals, he has written four other books: *The Poems and Translations of Sir Edward Sherburne (1616-1702), Introduced and Annotated* (Assen, 1961); *Fifty Psalms — An Attempt at a New Translation* (with Huub Oosterhuis and others; London, 1968; New York, 1969, 1974); *Christ Proclaimed — Christology as Rhetoric* (New York - Ramsey - Toronto, 1979); *Meditations in Glass — The Stained-Glass Windows of Saint John's Church, Bangor, Maine* (photography by J. Normand Martin; Bangor, Maine, 1981).

151